INCOME
INVESTING

INCOME INVESTING

An Intelligent Approach to Profiting from Bonds, Stocks, and Money Markets

JASON BRADY

New York   Chicago   San Francisco   Lisbon   London
Madrid   Mexico City   Milan   New Delhi   San Juan
Seoul   Singapore   Sydney   Toronto

1 2 3 4 5 6 7 8 9 0   QFR/QFR   1 8 7 6 5 4 3 2

ISBN: 978-0-07-179111-3
MHID: 0-07-179111-6

e-ISBN: 978-0-07-179112-0
e-MHID: 0-07-179112-4

This publication is designed to provide accurate and authoritative information in regard to the subject matter covered. It is sold with the understanding that neither the author nor the publisher is engaged in rendering legal, accounting, or other professional service. If legal advice or other expert assistance is required, the services of a competent professional person should be sought.
    —*From a Declaration of Principles Jointly Adopted by a Committee of the American Bar Association and a Committee of Publishers and Associations*

McGraw-Hill books are available at special quantity discounts to use as premiums and sales promotions, or for use in corporate training programs. To contact a representative, please e-mail us at bulksales@mcgraw-hill.com.

This book is printed on acid-free paper.

For H.M.S. Brady

CONTENTS

Prologue   **1**

1. Investing for Income   **5**
Slow, but Steady   6
Yield and Investor Psychology   9
Introduction to Asymmetry of Returns   11

2. Debt and the Cost of Money   **15**
The History of Debt and Money   15
What Is a Bond?   18
Duration: A Measure of Time and Sensitivity
to Change   19
The Yield Curve: The Price of Money for Different
Lengths of Time   23
When the Cost of Money Changes:
The Basic Economics of Interest Rates   26
The Federal Reserve   28
Key Economic Variables for Investors   31
Inflation versus Deflation, Today and Tomorrow   37

3. **The Wide World of Bonds: Types of Markets and How to Look at Them**   **43**

The Amazing Variety of Fixed Income   43

Credit Ratings: Let's Get This Out of the Way   47

The Trinity of Balance Sheets   52

Government Bonds: U.S. Treasuries, Foreign Governments, Municipal Bonds   52

Corporate Bonds   67

4. **Optionality and Selling the Upside**   **97**

Yield Is a Terrible Measure of Return   98

Options Basics   102

Optionality in Fixed Income   106

Effects of Optionality on Investment   111

Yield as a Cushion   116

Normal Distributions and Overconfidence   117

Correlation and Feedback Loops   126

Examples of Asset Classes and Products That Illustrate Optionality   134

5. **Equities for Income**   **145**

Upside Optionality and Volatility   148

Dividends versus Bond Yields   149

Dividend Payers Outperform   150

Go Global   153

It's Not Yield, It's Growth   155

Windstream versus China Mobile:
High Yield versus Growing Yield   158

Income from Stocks...for the Long Run   160

6. Banks: A Case Study   **165**
The Mechanics of a Bank Balance Sheet   166

Banks as Investors   168

Liquidity and Solvency   173

The Government Steps In   179

From Subprimes to Sovereigns: Banks in
Europe versus Banks in the U.S.   180

7. Toward a Sustainable Portfolio   **185**
Minksy's Financial Instability Hypothesis   186

Bottom Up: Margin of Safety   189

Top Down: The Market Environment   193

Portfolio Construction   194

Permanence of Capital   198

Reflexivity   200

Conclusion   202

Notes   **205**

Index   **209**

PROLOGUE

I struggled for some time trying to figure out both how "basic" to be and also how "deep" to get into various complex topics. It would be too easy to write a book that goes through the basic material on how bonds or dividend-paying stocks work and be done with it. Conversely, while getting into extreme depth on the math of bond, stock, and option valuation might be useful to a select few, it's really not the purpose of the present book. What I'd like to do here is present some basic topics and then build on those topics in a way that a reader who is educated in general but uninformed on the subject at hand can follow and understand. To this end, I've tried to make the tone of this book conversational and tried to anticipate as many questions and concerns as possible. If I haven't succeeded, I have only myself to blame.

In general I believe that people who are searching for knowledge are a pretty ideal audience. In addition, fixed income in particular seems to be, for most people, shrouded in mystery. In fact, bonds are pretty simple, and the required math to understand even complex topics is pretty easy. After all, we're talking about finance, not quantum physics. Finance needs to be, at the end of the day, simple enough for a lot of people to understand. If it isn't, you can't have a market (since a market is composed of more than just one person). What *is* complex is the way the market reacts to very simple financial inputs. So the complexity is not in the instruments themselves, but in market participants like you and me. To help understand why this is so, I've tried to make use of the work of various behavioral finance experts, as well as your, the reader's, common sense. Ultimately that common sense is the most important thing. You'll find, for example, that subprime mortgage Collateralized Debt Obligations (CDOs) are, when you have them dissected in front of you, pretty ridiculous. Yet markets were clamoring for more and more of this paper before the most recent recession. Nearly everyone thought they would work with no problems. Why?

Much of this book is devoted to a discussion of bonds, because that will always be a key source of income for most investors. Bonds have many virtues, even in today's low-interest-rate environment. I firmly believe that the two decades of solid stock returns from the early '80s to the dotcom boom taught (not without volatility) a generation of investors that "stocks for the long run" is a certain route to riches. The investment-advice industry and most individuals' innate optimism feeds into this asset allocation: I've never seen the average prediction for the market from a bunch of market strategists be anything other than 8–12 percent above the previous year's closing level. I've also never seen the Polyannas of stock investing, with their confidence in stocks always being successful in the long run, use the sample set of Japan over the last two decades, or many markets before World War II.

Analysts nearly always predict expanding profits, P/E ratios, or both. But of course we've seen over the past decade a very different reality. This is where bonds come in. If properly understood (part of what this book is for), bonds can be the ballast to your portfolio, while providing income and at least in part keeping you from depending solely on some greater fool to buy your stocks from you. Bonds also represent a huge variety of different risks, and as a result, flexibility in bond investment can be especially rewarding. Corporate bonds, the parallel to equities in the investment universe, represent only a small part of what is available in the bond marketplace.

But in all of this talk of bonds, I don't want to ignore stocks. I worry that the last decade's poor experience in equities and a seemingly insatiable demand for income have driven investors to finally seek a larger allocation in fixed income just when the likelihood of excellent fixed-income returns is low. We'll spend some significant time on the opportunity set that stocks represent in the income universe. Equities have some significant advantages over bonds, especially more recently. Bonds don't have the upside that equities do, and fixed income is called *fixed income* for a reason. Equities can grow their dividend, if management is both capable of producing growing profits and willing to share those profits with you, the investor.

So we'll talk about simple and complex kinds of income instruments, but we'll also talk about how to analyze them and how the markets for them are structured. Then we'll talk about their vulnerabilities, pitfalls, and why markets constantly seem to trip up rather than run smoothly. I hope that you'll enjoy the experience and, more important, that you will come away with a different mindset about investing for income, one that will help you be successful in reaching your long-term investment goals.

1

INVESTING FOR INCOME

"Amen!" cried Goodman Brown. "Say thy prayers, dear Faith, and go to bed at dusk, and no harm will come to thee."

—Nathaniel Hawthorne, "Young Goodman Brown"

If you've picked up a book about investing for income, I probably don't have to convince you that it's an important strategy or that income generation is likely to be a key part of investment returns for the foreseeable future. But coaxing income from your investment portfolio is easier said than done. There are a number of serious pitfalls and issues involved in any income strategy, and we'll explore them in depth as this book goes on.

Investing for income is not a new concept. John D. Rockefeller, famous philanthropist and founder of Standard Oil, reportedly said, "Do you know the only thing that gives me pleasure? It's to see my dividends coming in."[1] But investors do not need to be ultra-rich or even moderately wealthy to look toward their nest egg for income. Often this strategy is the basis behind retirement planning for all sorts of individuals and institutions. Endowments and foundations are designed to withdraw a certain percentage of their principal every year in order to meet their objectives, making an income strategy a perfect fit. Baby boomers are reaching the *disbursement stage,* or the stage at which they are no longer collecting wealth but using it, and as a result, the $17 trillion of investable assets in U.S. households will likely begin to skew toward income-producing assets and strategies.

SLOW, BUT STEADY

Market talking heads are typically interested only in what prices did today. I was invited to be on a particular financial news network a little while back and was asked what the "smart money" was buying "today." This is not the way to invest for income, or likely a successful way for most people to invest toward any goal.

At the end of 2011, something remarkable happened. The S&P 500's price was almost exactly the same at the end of the year as the beginning (down 4/100 of a point or .004 percent). News outlets everywhere reported that the S&P 500's return was zero for the year. "Virtually unchanged for the year,"[2] said Bloomberg News. But in fact, the total return on the index was 2.11 percent, because the S&P 500 pays a dividend (albeit a somewhat paltry one). Investors everywhere are quick to check the price return of all of their investments and forget the income that rolls in, unheralded, over the course of a longer investment time horizon.

With the greater availability of information these days, many investors check their account balances or the prices of what they own on a daily basis. Their mood is good or bad that day based on what direction those holdings went. Principally, investors are long on stocks, and therefore, when speaking with groups of investors, I can be fairly certain that they will be happy or sad based on the presence of green or red on the ticker running on the TV. Even if some people have a longer-term investment horizon (which, these days, means more than a year), they still are focused on price movements. Income is old fashioned and slow moving. If I own a stock that generates a 4 percent yield, that yield is likely going to be grossly overshadowed by the price movement of the stock over shorter periods of time. If people look at the stock price every day, it's easy to forget the dividend payment that comes along every quarter. But when that day comes, I'll receive my 1 percent. Of course, because the market incorporates that dividend payment into the price, it's likely that most investors will only notice the payment because the price of the stock went down by 1 percent that day. So it's very unsatisfying to an investor who is focused on returns on a day-to-day basis. Bonds are even worse in this regard, as prices are, for most fixed-income investments, more staid compared with the flashing red and green lights of stocks. And even when there is movement, the price of a bond is much less observable, making it much harder to celebrate winners or ignore losers.

Here's a quick thought experiment: Would you rather have a 5 percent yield for five years, or a series of returns that are: up 12 percent, up 10 percent, down 30 percent, up

35 percent, up 5 percent? Many people, at least when the whole series is presented, choose the latter. Though you have a 30 percent drawdown, it's mitigated by the up 35 percent the next year, and there are four winning years out of five. In fact, a 5 percent yield for five years is a 27.6 percent return. The irregular series of returns listed above is a 22.2 percent return. A significant difference, and with the irregular series you also had to deal with the heartache due to volatility and almost certainly the thought process of being in the market for the long run came up against some real angst.

Investing for income is a slow, steady race: a marathon, not a sprint. Though it's certainly exposed to market volatility, that stock that pays 4 percent in effect has a 4 percent tailwind. The bond fund that returns 5 percent, mainly through income gains, may not make fantastic gains in a stock bull market, but 5 percent compounded is pretty attractive. And that's the key: even if investors have a long time horizon, it's difficult for most people to think about compounding returns, geometric returns versus additive arithmetic ones. This is an advantage for investors who are willing to look past the daily ups and downs of the market and find true long-term returns. The investors who are supposedly in the market "for the long run" are often nevertheless scared away from the market just when they should be invested. It's hard to avoid that psychology. Because of the short-termism prevalent in investing today, the tortoise-like returns due to income get ignored by even conscientious, thoughtful market participants. If you look at your investments every day, the income doesn't show up.

Even every quarter, that income can be negligible (especially in today's low interest rate environment). But year in and year out, compounding income can be pretty interesting.

YIELD AND INVESTOR PSYCHOLOGY

Buying a bond or a dividend-paying stock for income is not the simple activity that it seems. Perhaps the act of buying the security itself is getting simpler, with significant advances in technology, but the various outcomes that can come from that activity are complex and fraught with potential ugliness.

A key to successful investment for income is to recognize what pitfalls are inherent in trying to coax a reliable income stream from an unreliable market. Investors (who are no different from any other type of person) are typically overconfident in their ability to anticipate all possible outcomes in a certain situation. Furthermore, the promise of a certain yield fixes the idea of that return in an investor's mind. Psychologists call this *anchoring.*

Amos Tversky and Daniel Kahneman, two pioneering researchers into cognitive biases, asked two groups of people to guess what percentage of African nations were in the United Nations. To the first group, they first asked if the number was more or less than 45 percent. To the second they first asked if it was more or less than 65 percent. The first group guessed a far lower percentage than the second, as they had been conditioned by the "anchor" of the suggested percentage from the previous question.[3]

The biggest problem in investing for income arises from the expectations of all of us as investors. Too many times people buy a security and believe that the quoted yield or expected income is something to bank on as a total return. Largely, that is not the case; yield is a bad measure of the potential for total return in almost all securities. Yield is what you can expect if everything about that security and the forces affecting it stay the same. It works if interest rates, credit spreads, and equity prices all don't move. But as any investor knows (at least intellectually), markets move all the time and over any time frame that you might wish to examine. I am lucky enough to run a series of funds and design strategies that are all designed to provide income for my shareholders and clients. Almost invariably, the first question I get from prospective investors about my funds is, "What is its yield?" It might be a reasonable starting point, but I haven't yet hit that notional yield as an exact return for any of my funds. The reason why investment firms are required to state that "Past performance is no guarantee of future results" is that too many people would assume that what has come before is likely to continue to happen. We may "know" that markets are volatile, but if we haven't felt that volatility recently, then we are less likely to believe that it can happen to us in the here and now.

The anchoring around a yield number has an even more pernicious effect than a mere suggestion of total return. If you are presented with two different investment options for income, and one has a higher yield than another, which are you more likely to choose? Certainly you can believe that the higher yield investment has more risk, but how much more? In good times, risk tends to recede into the background and reward comes forward. Markets are, of course, a battle between greed and fear, and income investments often throw that dichotomy into sharp relief. So if the world looks pretty rosy, people tend to choose the higher-yield investment and ignore the risk. Unlike a stock with no dividend, where your entire return is dependent on selling to a greater fool somewhere further down the line, the reward part of the equation with a high-yield bond is right in front of you. It's the yield, and it's staring at you, promising an immediate future filled with a fixed amount of money. Is it any surprise that investors reach for yield?

STOP THINKING ABOUT YIELD AS YOUR MEASURE OF INCOME.

INTRODUCTION TO ASYMMETRY OF RETURNS

Spectacular mishaps in the market seem to happen frequently, and recent history is just one example. We're currently experiencing a developed market sovereign crisis. The scars from Lehman Brothers' collapse are still fresh. The Enron/Worldcom/dotcom debacle was unpleasant. And all of this in the past decade! Large-scale market dislocations, or "hundred year floods" tend to happen much more frequently than models might predict. Nobel laureates and highly successful professionals still persistently believe that models will work and that today's sunny day will repeat tomorrow. Yet the violent market reactions seen as a result of European debt issues (specifically due to liquidity, in the case of Italy) is just the most recent upset that caused many carefully constructed models to be thrown out the window.

Of course I've detailed a number of negative events, but positive surprises are also out there. The fabulous advances in technology have powered a global productivity explosion. We want a portfolio that is exposed to upside surprises more than downside surprises. But looking more closely at income investments shows that, in general, it is the more negative result that you are stuck with. The most typical income investment is a bond. A typical corporate bond is a contract (or more simply, a loan) between the buyer of the bond (the lender) and the issuer of the bond (the borrower). The company may promise to pay 5 percent per year for ten years and then return the original notional amount at the end of the ten years. Now imagine that the company is spectacularly successful. The stock is soaring after a few years and continues to soar all the way through ten years. At the end of the ten years the company has ample money to pay you back. You are happy because you received what you were promised. Now look at the downside. The company is less successful. Its product is failing. It can't meet the contract (loan) terms that you had set out a few years before. Now it is in default, and you, the investor, are going to receive some fraction of your original investment. A typical defaulted corporate bond recovers 40 cents on the dollar. In the first case, you received a return of 5 percent. In the second case you lost 60 percent of your principal (though perhaps that loss is slightly softened by a few 5 percent coupon payments before the default). Bonds trade income (the 5 percent return) for upside (the stock moving up), and, though every investor works pretty hard to avoid the downside, sometimes bad things happen. Bonds have an asymmetric return profile, and that fact has a tremendous effect on how investors need to approach investing for income. We'll return to this idea at length in a later chapter.

The current income problem is outlined by Figure 1.1.

We've had several decades of lower and lower yields (along with low inflation). This has led to good returns from bonds, and frankly has also been a boon to stock investment. The year 2011 closed with the ten-year yield at 1.87 percent. How much lower can the ten-year go? If you are to commit to an investment time horizon of ten years (which is what

FIGURE 1.1 Ten-year U.S. Treasury yields.

investing in the ten-year presumes), do you believe that inflation will be low enough to make your real return (return after inflation), acceptable? After all, inflation at the end of 2011 was above 3 percent, so if inflation continues at its current level, you are currently committing to losing money. Where is the upside here?

Predicting the future of the market (and therefore the future of your income investments) is like trying to predict the weather several weeks, months, or years in advance. You might have a pretty good idea about what is very likely, and in fact today's sunny weather might make you feel confident in your prediction of further cloudless days. But hurricanes, tornadoes, and June blizzards can strike, and they strike more often than you might predict. What can cause more trouble is if the weather does indeed turn out to be sunny. Then you may leave your umbrella at home on the next day and get soaked.

This book tries to explore what might get you "soaked" when investing for income. At the very least, if it does rain, you can just hold it above your head.

2

DEBT AND THE COST OF MONEY

FAUSTUS: *Had I as many souls as there be stars*
I'd give them all for Mephastophilis.
By him I'll be great emperor of the world.
　　　　　　—Christopher Marlowe, *Dr. Faustus.*

THE HISTORY OF DEBT AND MONEY

Many people see the bond market as difficult to understand and its terms a strange foreign language. Stocks are simpler, with clearly identifiable prices in a market that rings a bell when it opens and closes. Fixed-income securities seem mysterious, with arcane concepts like duration and convexity and trade in a much less clearly defined market. But bonds are, by their essential nature, fairly uncomplicated. Most people have an experience with a bond, whether it is their mortgage, a small business loan from a bank, or a simple IOU due to a friend after forgetting a wallet during the lunch hour.

Anthropologist David Graeber has written a controversial account of the origin, history, and mechanics of debt. His conclusion, that debt is the engine of an unsustainable global system and that capitalism itself is doomed, does not convince me, but his unusual perspective on the relationship between money and credit is illuminating.

Interest-bearing debt began, according to Graeber, as a way of financing trade in Mesopotamian city-states:

> From quite early times, then, Temple administrators developed the habit of advancing goods to local merchants ... who would then go off and sell [them] overseas. Interest was just a way for the Temples to take their share of the resulting profits. However, once established, the principal seems to have quickly spread. Before long, we find not only commercial loans, but also consumer loans—usury in the classical sense of the term. By ca.2400 BC it already appears to have been common practice on the part of local officials, or wealthy merchants, to advance loans to peasants who were in financial trouble on collateral and begin to appropriate their possessions if they were unable to pay.[1]

On the "chicken or the egg" question of which came first, debt or money, Graeber writes:

> Money is not a commodity but an accounting tool. In other words, it is not a "thing" at all. Units of

currency are merely abstract units of measurement, and as the credit theorists correctly noted, historically, such abstract systems of accounting emerged long before the use of any particular token of exchange. The obvious next question is: If money is just a yardstick, what then does it measure? The answer was simple: debt.[2]

Graeber goes on to point out the trouble with IOUs and money as a measure of some debt is the question of why people would continue to put their faith in currency as a measure of value, an issue that is particularly in the spotlight at the moment, as many nations are eager to make their money less valuable in the belief that this will stimulate growth.

One of Graeber's general ideas is that debt, or a system of institutionalizing IOUs, actually came before money, and that money merely represents debt in some form. Interest is therefore actually the cost of that money, or the opportunity cost of not having the use of the money or the good that the money might represent. The concept of the cost of money is crucial to understanding the dynamics of debt. Sometimes the cost of money is high, for example, when there are many good available investing opportunities. Sometimes the cost of money is low, when the desire to invest or put money to productive use is low. We're here to talk about debt more concretely, but the concept of interest as the cost of money relates to the debt (or IOU, if you like) that money represents.

WHAT IS A BOND?

A bond is an obviously concrete and somewhat standardized form of debt. It is simply a contract that is issued with the expectation of principal repayment and can be thought of as an IOU. There is nearly always a fixed period of time for the contract and an interest rate stated or implied to compensate the lender for the use of his money for the given period. As an example, when you take out a mortgage from a bank, you have an interest rate (fixed or floating) and a time period to repay principal (usually over the course of 15 or 30 years). There are other complications (such as that the principal amortizes, meaning it gets paid off over time, rather than just at the end), but again this is effectively a contract between you and the bank. You can be sure that the bank put this loan on its book as an asset, and you are likely to feel quite strongly over time that the mortgage contract is a liability. We'll get to the math that is involved to determine the value of the mortgage asset to the bank (and to any investor in a mortgage), but this bond is simple in its essence.

Professionals value stocks with a variety of tools, including discounted cash flow analysis, comparables, and multiples of earnings or EBITDA (Earnings Before Interest, Taxes, Depreciation, and Amortization). But at the end of the day, to realize the value of your investment in a stock, you need to sell it to someone who would like to invest. The "greater fool" concept is that securities can continue to rise in value only if sellers can find "greater fools" that are willing to buy that stock at an ever greater price. Bonds have an advantage here: They mature. So in the most basic sense, investors don't need to value bonds in order to receive the benefits of ownership. As long as the contract holds up, the lender can sit back and receive interest payments and principal without finding a greater fool.

Inevitably, bond investors would like to be able to figure out the value of their holding before it matures, mostly because they'd like to sell before the bond makes its final payment. To understand how to value a bond, and by extension to understand how risky or sensitive a bond is to various market moves, *duration* is the first step.

DURATION: A MEASURE OF TIME AND SENSITIVITY TO CHANGE

Duration, simply, is the average length of time it will take an investor to get her money back. Surprised that duration, that complex bond-geek term, is just a length of time? Not so complex is it? Welcome to the not-very-arcane world of bonds. Still, let's dig a bit deeper. You could easily deduce, by the above definition, that bonds that mature over a longer period of time (say a mortgage that has a 30-year term versus one with a 15-year term) might have a longer duration, right? But what does that mean to you as an investor in terms of risk?

Let's imagine two securities. The first is one in which you invest $100 in a one-day (called overnight) bond. You are offered the going rate for that investment, say 5 percent. That 5 percent is actually an annualized number, so you'll

actually receive far less than that for your overnight investment, though if you continued to invest for an entire year in
that same security every day you'd eventually receive your $5
on your $100. For the second security, instead of lending over-
night, you lend for ten years at the same 5 percent rate. In this
case, you are "locking in" a 5 percent rate for ten years, so that
after a year you will receive $5 on your $100 investment, and
indeed you will continue to receive that $5 every year for ten
years, provided that you hold onto this bond.

Now imagine that the going rate for both investments
changes the moment after you buy your two securities.
Instead of 5 percent, the going rate becomes 1 percent. What
is the effect on the price of each one of your holdings? For
the overnight security, you are looking at reinvesting the next
day, and instead of getting that $5 by repeating the trade every
day for a year, you're going to be stuck with a series of investments that will net you $1. That is much less appealing than
what is happening with your second, longer security. The
ten-year security is "locked in" at 5 percent. But the going
rate on a new ten-year security is now 1 percent. The value
of that 5 percent income stream just went higher because the
new cost of money is lower. So *longer* duration securities *rise
more* in value when *interest rates fall*. Similarly, *shorter* duration securities *rise less* in value when *interest rates fall*.

Of course, the opposite is true. Imagine instead of the
interest rate going from 5 percent to 1 percent, it rises to
10 percent. Now that overnight investment looks a bit better,
because you can immediately reinvest at a higher rate when

the bond matures, whereas for the longer-term security you are "locked in" (that term suddenly has a more unpleasant connotation) to a lower rate. So *longer* duration securities *fall more* in value when *interest rates rise*. Figure 2.1 shows you the change in price for a given change in yield for various maturities of bonds.

So duration is not just a measure of the length of time it will take for you to get your money back as an investor, it is also a measure of your exposure to changes in interest rates. On the flip side of interest rate risk is what is called reinvestment risk. Because it is likely that you are going to buy something else to continue to receive some sort of income stream, you are exposed to the possibility that what you will be reinvesting in will have a lower, less attractive rate. Basically,

FIGURE 2.1 Duration: Changes in bond prices of various maturities with changes in yield.

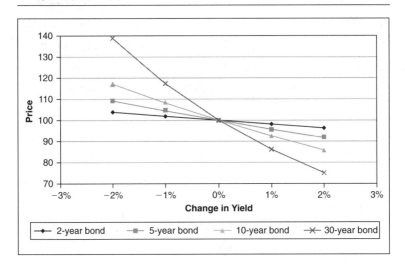

if interest rates go up and you have "locked in" a lower rate, people would say that you are exposed to interest rate risk. When you have the overnight bond and interest rates go down, people would say that you're exposed to reinvestment risk. Of course you were exposed to both, but people only consider the risks they are taking when things go wrong.

Finally, just a little bit of math. Duration is a simple concept, but it's also a powerful tool for determining the exact risk that a certain security has after a certain change in interest rates. The simple equation is that the price movement of a bond for a given change in rates is equal to the duration of that bond multiplied by the change in rates.

$$\text{Price Change} = \text{Duration} \times \text{Interest Rate Change}$$

So a bond with a ten-year duration moves 10 percent down in price when interest rates move up 1 percent. This doesn't include the income stream coming from the bond, but it gives you a general idea of how exposed an investment might be to rate change. If you add in the income stream, you can get an idea of the total return of a bond over a certain period of time. Say that ten-year duration bond has a 5 percent coupon (as in our earlier example). If rates move up 1 percent over the course of a year, your total return is approximately negative 5 percent: negative 10 percent from the price change, and positive 5 percent from the coupon. This is an example of something we'll talk about later, which is your income stream or coupon as the cushion against adverse events.

A quick note: the word *duration* is nearly always used to refer to a bond's sensitivity to "risk-free" interest rates only. But bonds can have duration exposure that relates to other rates. The math of duration works no matter whether the rate that is changing is risk-free interest rates or credit spreads. Risky bonds pay more than risk-free bonds, and the difference is spread. If that spread rises 1 percent and the risk-free rate stays the same, the typical fixed-coupon bond will lose exactly the same amount as if the spread stayed the same and the risk-free rate rose 1 percent. When market participants are looking at the change in price for a bond relative to a change in spread, the term that they use is *spread duration*. This stuff really isn't that complicated.

THE YIELD CURVE: THE PRICE OF MONEY FOR DIFFERENT LENGTHS OF TIME

A casual glance at the cost of money—interest rates—over different time frames will reveal that there are generally, often wildly, different rates over different time periods. The *yield curve* is a term that implies the differences in yield over varying time frames. See Table 2.1 and Figure 2.2.

There are several proposed reasons for why money might cost different amounts over different time frames, and going through them briefly should help solidify a number of the concepts we've discussed previously.

We've already talked about the difference between the interest rate risk of shorter-term securities versus that of

TABLE 2.1 Yield Curve

Date	2	5	10	30
12/29/11	0.27	0.91	1.92	.30
12/31/10	0.60	2.01	3.30	4.33
3/29/06	3.03	4.30	5.05	5.47

FIGURE 2.2 The Yield Curve: The cost of money for different lengths of time.

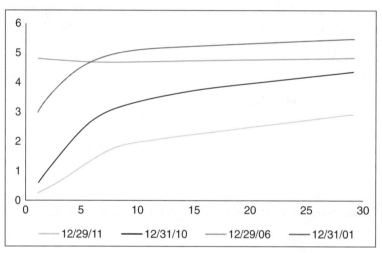

Source: Bloomberg

longer-term securities. Given the existence of significant uncertainty, investors generally expect more payment for committing money over a long term. The idea of *liquidity preference* is that the shorter-term investment is more flexible because you get your money back more quickly. As a result, yield curves are generally upwardly sloping, which just means that money costs less over a short term and more over a longer term.

Another key reason why yield curves are various shapes is due to *expectations* of future rates. If short-term rates are especially low and are expected to go higher in the next several years, it's reasonable to expect that money will cost significantly more for a longer period of time. If the yield curve were not upwardly sloping in this case, an investor could take advantage by selling longer-term securities (or borrowing money) at lower long-term rates while at the same time buying shorter-term securities (lending money) at the short-term rate. When the short-term loan came due, the investor could relend money at the now higher rate, while at the same time enjoying the locked-in lower rate on his longer-term borrowed money. In fact, some fixed-income investors do this exact trade if they believe that rates are going up faster than the market expects. Going back to our discussion of duration, the sold longer-term security would go down significantly in price in a rising-rate environment, while the bought shorter-term security would go down much less, thereby yielding a profit to the investor.

All this is to say that expectations of future rates have a dramatic effect on the shape of the yield curve. In general, if a yield curve is "steep" (front-end rates are much lower than long-term rates), the market expects rates to rise over the medium to long term. Conversely, if the yield curve is "flat" (front-end rates are the same as long-term rates) or "inverted" (front-end rates are actually higher than long-term rates), the market expects that rates generally will fall over time.

One last reason for yield curve shapes is that different investors have different reasons for investing in different parts of the yield curve. Because banks borrow from their depositors, who can often remove that money at the blink of an eye, banks don't like to invest over very long periods. Life insurance companies, on the other hand, know that they are going to be paying out benefits over a very long period of time, and so they naturally prefer longer-term securities. Because interest rates are the result of supply and demand, different sources of that supply (as well as different sources of demand) can change rates at various points along the yield curve. This is often referred to as the "preferred habitat" theory.

An important corollary to all of this is that different interest rates change at different rates, and while duration is a good tool for determining the interest rate risk of a certain security, it's not a complete picture of the risk as you must figure out *which* rate is moving in addition to *how much* it might move.

WHEN THE COST OF MONEY CHANGES: THE BASIC ECONOMICS OF INTEREST RATES

So if duration is a measure of exposure to interest rate changes, why do interest rates change, and under what conditions should investors be more concerned with rates going higher (interest rate risk, be scared of owning longer duration) or lower (reinvestment risk, be scared of owning shorter duration)? Remember, interest rates just represent the cost of money. Anyone who has taken a basic course in economics or who has thought about markets of any kind understands that markets operate on the basis of supply and demand. When a certain good is in high demand and has a low supply, the cost of that good goes up. Money is the same way. If money is in demand and in low supply, the cost of money rises. The conditions that might lead to money being in demand is when an economy is growing and there is a great demand for borrowing for expansion. If you own a business and you'd like to expand, maybe you don't have the money on hand to add a wing to your restaurant. However, with reservations piling up, you feel you could easily serve more people per night, if only you had the money to expand into the space next door. Well, perhaps the economy in general is humming along and part of the demand for your restaurant's food is an expression of the confidence that goes along with an expanding economy. "Hey kids, let's all go out for dinner tonight!" So you, the budding restaurateur, go to the bank for a loan in order to expand. But the economy is clipping along nicely, remember, so you have to get in line. By the time you talk to a banker she has been besieged by similar requests the whole day and the banker only has a certain amount of deposits to lend. So the banker proposes a high rate of interest, because the banker's cash to lend is in high demand. Perhaps the rate of interest is so high that it makes your expansion idea uneconomical. But in any case, the demand for money has met a limited supply, and changed the cost of money to the point that the imbalance between supply and demand is rectified by the change in cost of money. So when economic conditions are good, oftentimes the costs of money (interest rates) go up.

As an investor in a bond, you are essentially in the role of the bank in the above story. You could put your money in a number of different investments, but you want to gain the best rate of interest possible. As an investor, often many different possible investments are vying for your dollar, and if there are more investments than there are dollars, frequently the cost of those investments must change, unless a greater supply of dollars comes to the party. In fixed-income investments, when there are more potential investments, the interest rate must rise to attract dollars (remember that interest rates and prices move in opposite directions).

Just as good economic environments lead to a great demand for money, weak economic environments often lead to much less demand for money.

THE FEDERAL RESERVE

Let's introduce an important actor in this whole drama of the changing cost of money. The Federal Reserve (the Fed) is an independent central bank that is charged with a dual mandate of maintaining price stability and low unemployment. Their primary tool for reaching these goals is a very powerful one. The Fed has control over the cost of money in the short term. The exact mechanism is a bit esoteric and is frankly not that important here, but suffice to say that the Fed can change the interest rate on overnight loans up and down by changing the supply of money. If money is in very high demand and the Fed would like to make money more available, it can do so.

Alternatively, if money is not in enough demand, it can change the supply to match the lower demand and thereby change the cost of money. The practical upshot of this is that the Fed can move short-term interest rates up and down. In this way it tries to regulate economic growth. If growth is too slow, the Fed tries to stimulate the economy by lowering interest rates. If growth is so fast that inflation is rearing its head, the Fed can raise rates to slow the demand for new loans and thereby slow economic growth. So on one hand the Fed tries to keep growth up so that unemployment stays low, but on the other hand because economies can overheat, the Fed can dampen that growth in order to keep inflation in check.

Although these changes in interest rates act with a noticeable and variable lag, the ability to change the cost of money is very important. As an investor in fixed-income securities, it's important to have a good idea of where the economy is going in order to decide if money will be in high or low demand.

So at the moment the Federal Reserve sees a world in which inflation is not too high and employment is not high enough. As a result, it is trying to increase the demand for money by making the cost of money very low. In fact, the Fed has made the cost of money in overnight markets essentially zero. As a borrower, this is great, because the price of money is very low. As an investor, however, this can be pretty frustrating. Because the biggest tool in the Fed's shed is the rate at the front end of the yield curve, investors in money market funds (which invest, by mandate, exclusively in the front end) are receiving next to nothing on their investments. This is by design. The Fed is looking to encourage investment further out the yield curve in longer-term securities, which, due to the steepness of the yield curve, pay much more. Thinking back to the *liquidity preference* idea, the Fed is really just looking for people to take more risk of any type; it just wants people to stop hiding in cash and cash-like securities such as the money market. So it makes those pay nothing. As a result, investors might make (and to a certain degree have made) money available for longer-term or generally riskier investments, which in turn should stimulate economic growth. By manipulating the cost of money, the Fed is trying to affect the speed of the economy.

The side effect of this, and other actions that the Fed is currently taking, is to make an environment which is quite favorable for borrowing money, but not necessarily for investing money. As an investor, the Fed is making the environment more difficult. Without this manipulation it's possible that shorter-term, less risky, securities would provide interesting income, as has been the case in the past. As an example, in 2006, the Fed had raised front-end rates to the point where the yield curve was inverted. Shorter-term investments paid more than longer-term ones, so an investor looking for yield did not have to take much duration risk (though the reinvestment risk of holding a portfolio of short-term securities was challenging). At that point, because the Fed was trying to keep the economy from overheating (unsuccessfully, as it turned out), fixed-income investments had better yields.

So when the Fed lowers rates, and fixed-income investments go up in price on a certain day, it's important to remember that, while you're reaping a one-day windfall, the environment for finding income more generally just got more difficult. At the same time, when rates rise, eventually, the fixed-income market will be crying foul as prices go down. But the environment for receiving income will have just improved.

The nearly zero percent interest rates that the Fed has created in the front end of the yield curve is not an acceptable long-run return for anyone, especially in the presence of inflation significantly higher than zero. Money-market investments have lost their allure, and, while safety will always have its attractions in a volatile world, investors have nevertheless responded to the Fed's actions by investing in riskier securities that they (and we all) hope will help to finance growth in the U.S. and global economy over time.

KEY ECONOMIC VARIABLES FOR INVESTORS

To help determine the value of the cost of money today and in the future, fixed-income professionals look at any number of different economic and market variables. Several of the most important of those variables are employment, inflation, and gross domestic product (GDP) growth. The first two variables are directly part of the Federal Reserve's mandate, and the third is really the Fed's key goal, so it's no surprise that these variables make up key parts of the environment for interest rates.

Employment conditions in any economy are crucial to understanding the health of that economy. Simply, if you have a job, you pay your bills and potentially invest and save.

If you don't have a job, you don't. If you have a job, you are producing something of value and paying taxes. The key indicator in the U.S. (and in many other markets) is the monthly jobs report. Every month on the first Friday of the month, the Bureau of Labor Statistics (part of the U.S. Department of Labor), releases figures on the unemployment rate, the number of new jobs gained or lost, and the aggregate hours worked. Often the jobs report can give important clues to how well the economy is performing. However, the rates are volatile, and therefore one month of data is never enough. Still, an accurate and thorough understanding of the state of employment in any economy gives investors a terrific window into the appropriate price for money. Usually, when unemployment is rising, the economy is doing poorly and interest rates are falling or are likely to fall. Similarly, when unemployment is falling, interest rates are usually rising.

Today's jobs picture is not good, in either the U.S. or other developed markets. When determining a reasonable rate of unemployment, most market observers consider that very high rates of unemployment often lead to low growth and deflation. Very low rates of unemployment can lead to inflation due to pressures on wages and the search for talent. Most economists believe that, for the U.S., the Non-Accelerating Inflation Rate of Unemployment (NAIRU) is around 6 percent. The unemployment rate in the U.S. has been well above this rate for some time.

The unemployment rate in the United States today may be underestimating the likely damage done by the 2008/2009 recession for two reasons: a declining labor force participation rate and underemployment. To understand these two reasons it's important to understand how the unemployment rate is calculated. The so-called "household survey" (so named because the interviewers call a selection of households—who said this fixed income stuff was complicated?) is performed by the Bureau of Labor Statistics by asking two key questions. First, "Are you employed?" If the answer is yes, great. If no, they ask a second question: "Are you looking for a job?" If the answer is yes, you are counted as unemployed. If the answer is no, you are not in the labor force. There are plenty of good reasons not to be in the labor force. You could be nine, or ninety years old, as an example. Still, the unemployment rate is the measure of those people who are not employed (no to the first question), but who are in the labor force (yes to the second question). In the last 40 years, the participation rate and production have increased greatly due to the bulge of the baby boomers and a similar boom in women entering the workforce. The latter has continued, but the former is changing significantly. As baby boomers retire, labor force participation is declining. Thus, even with an unchanged unemployment rate, the total number of employed and productive individuals is declining. This affects tax revenue and is a concern across the aging developed world, as the number of working-age individuals declines relative to the number of retired individuals. As you can see from Figure 2.3, even a recent decrease in the unemployment rate over the past couple of years has not led to any increase in employment.

FIGURE 2.3 A demographic headwind: the employment-to-population ratio.

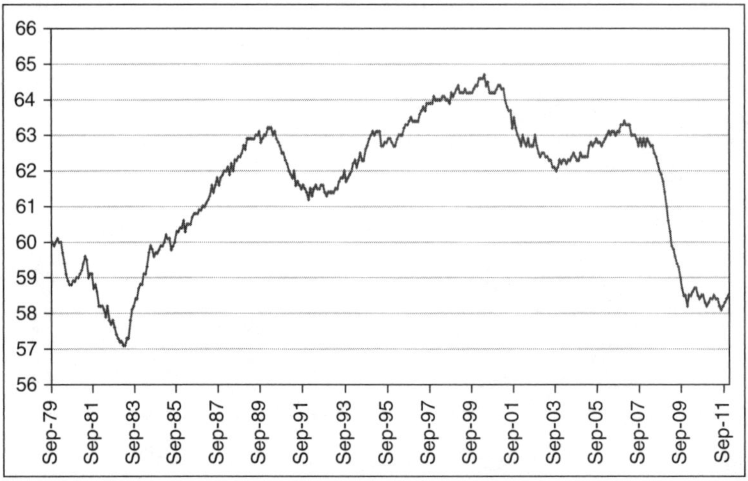

Source: Bloomberg

The degree of underemployment (as opposed to unemployment), in the United States and globally, is also an issue
now. Many investors look to the U6 rate (the Bureau of Labor
Statistics produces several measures of unemployment from
U1 to U6, with U6 being the broadest measure) produced by
the household survey that includes "total unemployed, plus
all persons marginally attached to the labor force, plus total
employed part time for economic reasons, as a percent of the
civilian labor force plus all persons marginally attached to the
labor force."[3] Many individuals are no longer searching for a
job because they have become discouraged by lack of success.
Other people are working part time "for economic reasons,"
meaning that they'd like to have full-time work, but can't find
it. As a result, the U6 number is about twice the often-quoted

headline unemployment rate (known to the Bureau of Labor Statistics as U3). Unemployment is a serious problem and represents significant slack in the economy.

The Federal Reserve, for what it's worth, is on the case. The Fed is one of the few central banks to have a dual mandate. Most central banks are only concerned with price stability, or balancing inflation and deflation. The Fed has an additional charge "to promote maximum employment." (This comes from the Federal Reserve Reform Act of 1977.) So if unemployment is rising, the Fed is likely to be acting by adding liquidity to the financial system in order to lower short-term interest rates. The opposite is also true, which at first seems odd. Wouldn't the Fed always want to increase employment and therefore stimulate the economy? Unfortunately, falling unemployment can also be the harbinger of inflation, which certainly threatens price stability.

Inflation, measured by both the Producer and Consumer Price Indices (PPI and CPI) are therefore key economic statistics for fixed-income investors. More important, inflation is a direct threat to the value of your income stream. If the dollar you're receiving buys 2 percent less next year than this year, you have to make more than 2 percent just to break even. Inflation is a treadmill for investors, and when it's running quickly, it's very hard for investors to keep up. The threat of ever-increasing inflation often causes investors to require ever higher interest rates in order to invest. It also has, in the past, caused ever higher demands by workers for higher wages. Both situations can be very damaging to the overall economic environment. Needless to say, income-oriented investors need to keep a sharp eye on inflation figures. We'll talk a bit more about inflation and deflation in a second.

Gross domestic product (GDP) growth is the last key indicator of economic health that investors need to understand. GDP is the measure of the output and spending of a particular economy. Because markets are more concerned with how conditions are changing versus how conditions currently are, the number everyone focuses on is GDP growth. (This is measured in the U.S. as an annualized percentage, but in many other economies the number is not annualized.) Most of the other economic indicators that appear over the course of the month or quarter are directly related to the components of the GDP calculation below.

$$GDP = Consumption + Investment + Government$$
$$Spending + Exports - Imports$$

One reason that GDP is not the sole focus of the market is that it comes quarterly, comes late, and is frequently revised. As an example, in the run up to the holiday season in late December, the Department of Commerce in the U.S. releases the third revision of the GDP for the *third* quarter. So, by the end of the year, we have reasonably firm numbers detailing what happened from July to September. Given that economic conditions can change significantly from one quarter to the next, this information is not current enough to be of immediate use. Still, the concept of the growth in output for an economy is crucial to understanding the prospects for individual income, employment, corporate profit growth, sovereign debt dynamics, and many other variables that directly affect investors' portfolios.

These measures of economic conditions are important in themselves, but in an increasingly global and interconnected economy, the interactions between economies have become equally important. Global trade is reflected in the GDP figure in the form of exports and imports, and the recent push by many countries, including the U.S., to become more export-based is, unfortunately, impossible. Many of the economic imbalances present in the world today are in part due to a significant import and consumption boom in developed markets, and a notable savings and export boom in developing markets, especially China. This has resulted in a large build up of reserves overseas, and these reserves have been recycled back into U.S. Treasury securities. As a result, more than half of the available stock of Treasury securities is held outside of the U.S., leading to vulnerabilities that we will discuss later.

INFLATION VERSUS DEFLATION, TODAY AND TOMORROW

A major debate is raging among economists about the prospect of deflation or inflation. A deflationary backdrop has dominated the global economy since the onset of the recession of 2008–2009, largely due to ongoing de-leveraging in the economy and a resultant decline in prices. Home prices are a great example: After growing dramatically on the back of easy lending practices through the middle part of the 2000s, home prices have since declined equally dramatically. This deflation has put pressure on borrowers, because many homes are now underwater (the borrowers owe more than the house is worth). Banks, also, are looking to shrink the size of their balance sheets due to large loan losses (and ongoing regulatory pressures). As a result, the leverage available to the economic system as a whole is declining. This is a headwind to GDP growth, as money that had previously been directed toward investment or consumption is instead being directed toward the repayment of debt. In a paper published in July 2010, James Bullard, President of the St. Louis Federal Reserve, wrote:

> The global economy continues to recover from the very sharp recession of 2008 and 2009. During the recovery, the U.S. economy is susceptible to negative shocks which may dampen inflation expectations. This could possibly push the economy into an unintended, low nominal interest rate steady state. Escape from such an outcome is problematic. Of course, we can hope that we do not encounter such shocks, and that further recovery turns out to be robust—but hope is not a strategy. The U.S is closer to a Japanese-style outcome today than at any time in recent history.[4]

Dr. Bullard's further conclusion was that significant further stimulus was warranted in order to forestall a recurrence of the deflationary spiral that still haunts the Japanese economy.

Alhough Dr. Bullard does not speak for the Federal Reserve, clearly with a policy of effectively zero percent interest rates and an ongoing effort to stimulate economic growth through the purchase of longer-duration assets, the Fed is obviously not particularly concerned with inflation. Given the change in the Fed's duration exposure due to "Operation Twist," whereby the Fed sold short-term bonds and bought long-term bonds, the Fed's equity capital would be wiped out with a relatively small change in long-term interest rates. In fact, Fed Chairman Ben Bernanke made a speech, while a Federal Reserve governor in 2002, in which he said that the Fed could and should pursue a number of unusual actions if it saw ongoing fundamental weakness. To illustrate the extreme tools available to the Fed, Bernanke suggested the possibility of throwing money from helicopters, thus earning him the nickname "Helicopter Ben." Less sensationally, with regard to the likelihood of deflation in the U.S., Bernanke said:

> *Like gold, U.S. dollars have value only to the extent that they are strictly limited in supply. But the U.S. government has a technology, called a printing press (or, today, its electronic equivalent), that allows it to produce as many U.S. dollars as it wishes at essentially no cost. By increasing the number of U.S. dollars in circulation, or even by credibly threatening to do so, the U.S. government can also reduce the value of a dollar in terms of goods and services, which is equivalent to raising the prices in dollars of those goods and services. We conclude that, under a paper-money*

system, a determined government can always gener-
ate higher spending and hence positive inflation.[5]

He went on, however, to talk about practical limits of inflationary policy. Nevertheless, the ability of the Fed to "print" money is an undeniable bulwark against deflation. (One note, however: the Fed on its Web site has as one of its Frequently Asked Questions, "Is the Federal Reserve printing money in order to buy Treasury securities?" They conclude, despite Bernanke's speech, that the answer is, "No.")

One further note around the incentive structure that the Federal Reserve has with regard to inflation versus deflation: Deflation hurts borrowers. Right now, in the U.S., there is a preponderance of borrowers, including the U.S. Treasury. As a result, there is great incentive to avoid deflation and, indeed, create some inflation.

While the Fed is currently unconcerned about the prospect of inflation due to excess stimulus, the much-lauded previous Chairman of the Federal Reserve Board Alan Greenspan dramatically disagrees with the course of action being taken by Bernanke, Bullard, and their cohorts. He wrote in mid-2010 that:

The U.S. government can create dollars at will
to meet any obligation, and it will doubtless con-
tinue to do so. U.S. Treasurys are thus free of credit
risk. But they are not free of interest rate risk. If Trea-
sury net debt issuance were to double overnight, for

*example, newly issued Treasury securities would con-
tinue free of credit risk, but the Treasury would have to
pay much higher interest rates to market its newly
issued securities. I grant that low long-term interest
rates could continue for months, or even well into next
year. But just as easily, long-term rate increases can
emerge with unexpected suddenness. Between early
October 1979 and late February 1980, for example,
the yield on the ten-year note rose almost four percentage points.*[6]

Thus the former and current Federal Reserve Chairmen
agree about the ability of the Fed to create inflation, but disagree on the likely results. These two individuals no doubt
are intelligent, very well educated, and extraordinarily well
informed. The fact that they disagree so dramatically tells me
that the question is not an easy one to answer. Yet it's a crucially important question for determining the future cost of
money and thereby the future price on fixed income securities. If we are unable to overcome the deflationary pressures
brought on by significant economic slack, then low interest rates are likely to persist for the foreseeable future, and
James Bullard's concerns about a Japanese-style outcome are
warranted. On the other hand, if the massive monetary
stimulus that the Fed has introduced works too well and
Greenspan's fears are realized, interest rates will rise dramatically, and many bond investors will lose money due to their
duration exposure.

Ultimately, given the fluid nature of the current economic environment, investors should be prepared for any eventuality. Though markets are always challenging, even Ben Bernanke called the current economic environment, "usually uncertain."[7]

3

THE WIDE WORLD OF BONDS: TYPES OF MARKETS AND HOW TO LOOK AT THEM

I have seen them, gentle, tame, and meek,
That now are wild, and do not remember
That sometime they put themselves in danger
To take bread at my hand; and now they range,
Busily seeking with a continual change.

         —Sir Thomas Wyatt, "They Flee from Me"

THE AMAZING VARIETY OF FIXED INCOME

Fixed income is often considered, in an odd juxtaposition, both difficult to figure out and boring. Equity markets hold appeal for many investors because of the ownership stake that holders have. But bonds, with their geeky equations and their generally lesser volatility, are the purview of the accountants of the investing world, bond fund managers.

Maybe the above is true, and I'm just hopelessly biased. But while I think equities have tremendously valuable attributes and are endlessly fascinating (we'll talk at greater length about them in a bit), they deal with one type of investment. Equity investors may look at many different variables, but ultimately they are stuck in examining the health and earnings power of corporations. Corporate bonds are merely one kind of fixed-income security, and not even the most common. Bond markets range from simple structures backed by very creditworthy institutions (like the U.S. government), to complex series of cash flows backed by uncertain revenues from odd projects (that sounds like a stock, come to think of it). The global fixed-income market is something like $65,000,000,000,000 in size (that's 65 trillion dollars), which is about double the size of the equity market. Those bonds are of many shapes and sizes. As a consequence, it's interesting to look at some broad categories of fixed income and explore their general characteristics in order to get a general feeling of what is available to fixed-income investors.

Let's start with the broader differences between stocks and bonds. We've already discussed the idea of bonds as contracts. But the way that they trade is also important. Stocks prices are quoted freely, and the difficulty for an individual investor to trade one share is less than that for institutional investors, who must piece out their sales and slowly collect their total purchases. Discount brokerages these days offer very low-cost trades and good execution, such that even small buys and sells are reasonably cost effective. (The fact that this may lead to greater trading is exemplified by the tone of the advertisements that I see: "Trade at XYZ brokerage from anywhere! Even while out running or biking, or from an airport!" I'm not sure you make your best investment decisions with the information available on your phone's screen.) No one argues about where stocks are, even if an institutional investor would have to trade out of its shares over the course of a week or two.

Bonds on the other hand, trade "over the counter," which just means that they don't have an exchange where prices get posted. In the U.S., the National Association of Securities Dealers (NASD) has started a system called Trade Reporting and Compliance Engine (TRACE) that posts prices for a number of bonds. But that's beside the point. The real issue is that smaller sizes of bonds are likely to receive a worse price in the market relative to larger sizes. In fact, "odd lots," as smaller sizes are known, are typically anything less than $1 million in the principal amount of bonds. The reason for this is that large institutions, like insurance companies, mutual funds, hedge funds, and pension funds are by far the biggest participants in the bond markets, and, away from municipal bonds, there are, relative to stocks, very few retail participants. An institution with hundreds of millions, even tens of billions of dollars to spend is not going to bother with sizes that don't help them in their investment strategy. As a result, individuals trying to purchase bonds in smaller sizes face an uphill battle. With stocks, a market maker might take an order to execute a stock trade in the context of a market that is trading in significant size. Verizon has one stock, but hundreds of bond issues. Goldman Sachs also has one stock, but thousands of different bonds. So an individual bond might not trade for days or weeks. When a market maker takes an order to trade a particular bond, it's very unlikely that she will find the other side of the trade immediately. There just aren't enough trades. So the market maker will take bonds into inventory. Unlike broker-dealers in the stock market, who take a commission to trade with the market, fixed-income market makers buy on the *bid* and sell on the *offer*. When asked to buy bonds, they try to purchase them at a price that is low enough that they can be reasonably assured of a profit when they try to resell that bond. When a bond is very liquid—when there are many trades—market makers can be relatively aggressive in their bids and offers, so that the spread between the two is reasonably small. U.S. Treasury securities trade very frequently, and therefore the bid-ask spreads for Treasuries are very small. In fact, U.S. Treasuries are one of the few bond asset classes where retail investors can expect to receive good prices on both a buy and a sell of any size. More esoteric securities are likely to have a much higher bid-ask spread. It is not unusual to see the bid-ask spread for a $100 face amount bond be as much as $1 in normal situations and up to $10 or more when news is out or when there are particularly poor market conditions.

Lately liquidity in many markets has been drying up. This is partly due to the cyclically poor performance of risky securities and the lack of desire that investment banks have to provide bids and offers to the marketplace. But there is potentially a structural, longer-lasting component as well.

As broker-dealers within banks get more highly regulated, their ability to take risk in the form of providing bids and offers is likely to go down. The "Volcker Rule" as part of the Dodd-Frank legislation that was recently passed, forbids banks to take proprietary risk. This could mean that banks can only act as agents to facilitate trades. In equity markets, this isn't much of a problem, because, aside from certain block trades, most banks are acting as agents anyway, buying and selling stock in small pieces with the market. Also, U.S. Treasury volume is very large, and therefore matching buyers and sellers in a short period of time is easier. Treasury traders have the option, every day, to go home without any positions. But smaller markets like those for high-yield corporate bonds or nonagency mortgages are much less liquid. To facilitate trades, broker-dealers take positions without having another side to the trade. The line between taking a position to facilitate a trade and having a proprietary position is impossibly thin. It remains to be seen how far regulators will push this line. If liquidity gets worse, investors can expect much higher volatility in the marketplace.

CREDIT RATINGS: LET'S GET THIS OUT OF THE WAY

Credit rating agencies are, as was amply demonstrated in the most recent crisis, quite fallible. However, these hardworking people generally give their honest assessment of a credit. This was, and is, more often true in corporate credit than in say, structured product such as nonagency mortgages, CDOs, and the like, because the information is less opaque and the structure of the bond itself is simpler. So, often credit rating agencies can be a valuable extra set of eyes when examining a particular bond. If you have access to the reports, they will usually set out in broad terms many of the basics of a certain entity's financial condition, as well as a quick view of the challenges and opportunities that entity (be it a company, government, or financial construction) may experience which could change the rating. Again, it's just another set of eyes.

Ratings agencies generally rank bonds according to a scale from nearly unimpeachable to actually in default. Each rating agency has a slightly different nomenclature, but generally the scale looks as follows (this is the usage of Standard & Poor's):

AAA
AA
A
BBB
BB
B
CCC
CC
C
D

Each letter rating also has the possibility of a + or a −, leading to such gradations as A+, A, and A− within the overall

A category (only the top and bottom rungs are exceptions). Ratings that are BBB– and above are, by convention, considered to be *investment grade,* whereas those that are BB+ and below are considered to be *speculative grade* or just plain junk. The probability of default does not increase linearly for most asset classes. In corporate bonds, for example, the probability of default at the AAA level over five years is nearly zero and at the CCC to C level is nearly 50 percent.[1] Of course this should lead to very different levels of payment for each different rating category. The question that every investor asks is: "How much?" The cost of money for the risk of credit (as well as the risk of time as in duration calculation) is at the heart of this and determines the price of the bond.

Unfortunately, rating agencies face a number of constraints when trying to determine and disseminate appropriate ratings. The first is that not all kinds of borrowers have the same kinds of risk. We'll talk about the various different kinds of bonds shortly, but suffice to say that a mortgage obligation has a different risk profile than a government bond or a corporate bond. The second problem that rating agencies have is that they assess a borrower with a certain letter rating regardless of the length of time of the borrowing in question. When trading corporate bonds in the early 2000s, I recall that there was some significant question around AT&T's ability to pay its long-term debt. At the time, AT&T was a shell of its former self, having sold off its wireless business and its cable business, among other divestitures. The wireline, or "land line" business was obviously declining, and there seemed to be little hope for the company over a longer term. Still, the company had significant cash and ongoing cash flow. But its 30-year debt and its three-year debt were, by convention, rated the same way.

The last, and most important, issue that rating agencies have is a more philosophical problem (and one we'll get into in great detail toward the end of this book). Rating agencies' ratings are supposed to be a long-term look at the credit quality of a borrowing entity. The analysts there obviously try to take into account the various situations the borrower might encounter through the course of its rated life. But the analysts cannot and can never envision the full range of possibilities in an ever-changing global economy. Highly rated entities can't get much more highly rated, yet the "investment grade" imprimatur indicates that there is sufficient cushion against many, or nearly all, eventualities. If the situation gets better, the rating stays high. If it gets worse … oops. As such, ratings can never be strictly correct, they are only an indicator of present condition. One of the most telling examples of this problem is that, before 2008, structured-finance professionals would crow about how various forms of asset-backed securities tended to have ratings transitions that were largely positive. In other words, the bonds tended to move up in ratings through their life. Corporate bonds, on the other hand, nearly always have negative ratings transitions. Entire investment strategies were built on the idea that structured products moved up in ratings. Again, oops.

But rating agencies would not have the same effect on the market if their opinions were taken as just that. Really the trouble comes when markets institutionalize these ratings. As an example, the current European sovereign debt crisis has ratings as a source of instability, given the requirement of many charters to invest or lend against only credits of high quality. The European Central Bank has had to discard restrictions around the ratings of sovereign bonds it will take as collateral. Discussions of a "Eurobond"—a security referencing as a guarantor all the nations in the Euro—are hung up in part due to how to achieve a AAA rating and what would happen if that rating were to change for the worse. Mortgage-backed securities can fail to pay all principal back but have very good payment profiles, yet the same investors who bought those securities for nearly zero yield when they were AAA will be both unwilling and unable to buy them when they generate a much higher, and equally certain, income stream.

The downgrade of U.S. Treasuries may be the beginning of the end of rating-agency power, because the market still recognizes the great strengths of the U.S. economy and the U.S. financial system, especially on a comparative basis. But I doubt it. All markets are looking for shortcuts, and a rating is an easy shortcut compared to doing your own credit work. In aggregate, the ratings are pretty good for some assets, and that gives the rating agencies enough legitimacy to keep going. Everyone wants to be able to monitor credit quality without looking at individual issuers, and ratings are convenient. So we can rail against their power, their lack of foresight, and their contribution to the latest recession and market meltdown, but I doubt that we will truly rid ourselves of them; the market is too lazy.

THE TRINITY OF BALANCE SHEETS

The fixed-income market is effectively categorized by different types of balance sheets. Investors have a choice between government bonds (e.g., U.S. Treasuries, California state municipal bonds, Malaysian government bonds priced in ringgit), corporate bonds (Verizon, Goldman Sachs, Finmeccanica), and bonds referring to individual credits (U.S. mortgages, credit card loans, car loans). Let's take them one by one.

GOVERNMENT BONDS: U.S. TREASURIES, FOREIGN GOVERNMENTS, MUNICIPAL BONDS

When you buy a government bond, there often is the taxing authority backing that bond. So in theory, the government has the ability to pay you back. If the government gets into trouble, it just raises taxes on its constituents. At least that's the theory. What we're seeing now in Europe is that the willingness of a government to continue to tax its constituency is reasonably proportional to the constituency's willingness to pay that tax. So it's not a question of ability, it really comes down to willingness. But in general, government bond markets are the first ones that investors come across, due to their size, liquidity, and visibility.

U.S. Treasuries

When investors think of "bonds," at least in the U.S., most people think about U.S. Treasuries. Treasuries are a pretty basic investment, in that most (but not all) have very simple structures. T-Bills are short-term and are priced with a zero coupon at a discount. For a typical $1,000 bill you may invest $999 and receive $1,000 a short while later, though in the current market the amount investors commit to receive $1,000 is closer to $999.90. T-Notes are intermediate-term obligations that have a coupon and pay semiannually. T-Bonds are just longer-term versions of T-Notes and are most typically referenced 30-year bonds. U.S. Treasuries, in addition to being relatively simple in structure, also represent quite a large market. The outstanding U.S. Treasury market, ex-Bills, is about $9 trillion, up from $3.4 trillion in 2000. Furthermore, the U.S. government has long been considered the best credit available. As a result, the U.S. Treasury market is considered a benchmark for many other markets. It is one of the most liquid markets in the world, where investors don't blink an eye to trade hundreds of millions of dollars in a single trade and where hundreds of billions trade on a daily basis. This liquidity, and the perception of high credit quality, means that U.S. Treasury rates are considered the "risk-free" rate and those rates are indeed incorporated into many models.

Treasuries have for some time been the true "gold standard" of fixed-income investment (the irony being that the U.S. government took the dollar off of the gold standard in the 1970s). But in August of 2011, S&P downgraded U.S. Treasury securities, challenging the perceived wisdom that the securities were risk-free. Subsequently, yields on Treasuries actually moved lower. The rationale, while perhaps counterintuitive, is not tremendously odd. If Treasuries are to be considered risky from a credit perspective, what are we to say about troubled European banks, Chinese property companies, or indeed any risky endeavor? Likely we should be more concerned about those. In addition, if the U.S. is to correct its imbalances (principally its budget deficit), that is likely to involve painful decisions that are detrimental to growth. So, rather than sell the downgraded security, go look for securities that represent very low-risk propositions that will be a safe haven in times of trouble. Hence, buy U.S. Treasuries.

At the end of the day, Treasuries are liquid, high quality, and simple. Their availability may call into question their quality given the recent willingness of the U.S. government to spend dramatically more than it takes in, but they retain their status of a quality investment.

Current Federal Reserve Policy and Its Effect on Treasuries

Current Federal Reserve policy is to keep rates at very low levels, and the Fed is achieving this, not only through a very low Fed Funds rate, but also through purchases of longer-term fixed-income instruments. This second policy is very unusual, and has been given the moniker "quantitative easing" due to the fixed quantity of securities the Fed has committed to buy. Because the Fed has access to unlimited quantities of U.S. Dollars (they control the printing presses), this has two effects. First, it adds money to the financial system, which, in a recession, typically doesn't have a lot of money being put to work. In fact, investors, from individuals to banks, are putting money in the proverbial mattress (in some cases including T-Bills yielding literally zero) and exacerbating an already slowing lending environment. So the Fed is trying to get more money in the system to juice the economy and further encourage a more healthy lending environment. The other effect of the Fed's purchases and low rates is to discourage investors from buying Treasuries by lowering their interest rate. The Fed is such a large potential buyer that, even though the U.S. Treasury is spending much more than it's bringing in, rates remain low. In fact, rates are so low that the rate of interest paid on most Treasuries is currently notably below the current rate of inflation.

If inflation continues to be as high as it is today, investors are locking in real losses. Though their nominal money will increase, because interest rates are somewhat higher than zero, their real purchasing power will erode because inflation is higher than the current interest rate. Furthermore, many observers, including former Fed officials, believe that a higher rate of inflation will help to dig the over-indebted housing market (and U.S. Treasury) out of their hole. Therefore, these officials are encouraging the Fed to allow a higher rate of inflation than their typical implied 2 percent target. But even if the 2 percent number holds, the Treasury yield curve will hand investors negative real returns. And this is before taxes on the interest! The only scenario where investors will make out well with Treasuries, particularly longer-duration Treasuries, given the current rates on offer, is if the U.S. enters a prolonged period of deflation and recession. In effect, the U.S. needs to follow the path of Japan.

The U.S. Treasury has issued (along with several other governments and a few corporations), bonds that are linked to inflation. In the U.S., these bonds are called TIPS (Treasury Inflation Protected Securities), though globally this type of bond is called a *linker,* due to its link to an inflation index. While this security's structure would help, relative to nonlinked "nominal" Treasuries, the inflation index must reflect the investor's actual inflation experience in order to avoid negative real returns. In the U.S., the Consumer Price Index (CPI) is used to adjust the principal amount of TIPS to increase the value of the bond in keeping with inflation. Many investors have found their costs increase at a much higher rate than CPI, due to the vagaries of the CPI's calculation method. In addition, the current interest rate for TIPS is actually negative for bonds maturing inside of ten years. Thus, though the buyer of TIPS is protected somewhat from a high inflation scenario, that same investor is locking in a certain nominal loss, no matter what the path of inflation becomes. In general, because of the poor track record of riskier assets over the course of the past decade, those seeking to put their money with the "risk-free" U.S. Treasury are not receiving much in return.

Other Sovereign-Government Bonds

While U.S. Treasuries hold a preeminent place in the world of fixed income, other governments also sell debt to finance their budgets. German bonds hold a place within the European marketplace similar to U.S. Treasuries, and is typically the benchmark against which other bonds (government or otherwise) are compared for the euro-denominated market. Japanese and Italian bonds have significant markets (second and third in size to U.S. Treasuries) and as a direct consequence are widely held. However, neither market has the same benchmark status. Over 90 percent of Japanese bonds are held by domestic Japanese, which makes that market's dependence on foreign buyers very low and also reduces the Japanese Government Bond (JGB) market's importance outside of Japan. In addition, though the yields on JGBs are very low (and have been for well over a decade), there are burgeoning concerns around a government that has a gross debt to GDP ratio above 200 percent. It seems as though the only reason the market has not exploded to dramatically higher yields (thus almost surely rendering the Japanese government bankrupt given huge interest costs) is the proportion of domestic holders who are prodigious savers and therefore sustain a very large buyer base for the bonds.

The global debt market is dominated by these developed economies and debts denominated in their currencies. In fact, debt in the currencies of the U.S. dollar, the euro, the British pound, and the yen account for well over 90 percent of the available debt markets. While other markets are growing, these remain in their infancy. One reason for this is that debt markets, to be effective, require a well developed and tested set of contract laws. Investors must be comfortable with both the investment case and the legal jurisdiction of a particular local currency bond, and it is only recently that this has occurred. Despite significant recent flows of money into local currency markets, to be sustainable these markets really require local buyers. These buyers, typically pension funds, local insurance companies, and local banks, are often slow to develop.

The roles of developed- and developing-market countries have seemingly swapped in recent years. Japan has a very high debt to GDP ratio. Italy has a similar debt to GDP problem and something of a similar domestic buyer base, but enough debt is held outside of the hands of Italian savers that there has been significant recent concern about the sustainability of Italy's debt, and indeed the problems of excessive debt of many Eurozone countries. Those problems, which are shared by other developed markets' economies (like the U.S. and Japan), include both a large primary deficit (money spent more than money earned before interest costs) and a difficult demographic situation as it relates to entitlements. With regard to the primary deficit, governments everywhere often spend much more than they make in recessions, due to both a dramatic increase in stimulative programs and a sudden shrinkage of GDP, though interestingly, Italy's primary deficit today is much better than most other developed markets. Debt to GDP ratios skyrocket, because the debt numerator is going up while the GDP denominator is going down.

The above dynamic regarding growth, spending, and the cost of debt is not new. What's new is that it is occurring in large, developed markets, as opposed to smaller, developing ones. Argentina experienced this issue and defaulted on its debt early in this century. Indeed so called "emerging market" economies have often had significant debt problems. Their debt concerns stemmed in part from their dependence on foreign capital to fund high growth. Unfortunately, when growth didn't occur in a straight line, the willingness of foreign money to hang around in the tough times was pretty low. So economic growth in emerging markets has been more volatile than in developed markets with more stable lending conditions. Other reasons for past trouble in emerging markets include corruption, poor monetary policies, runaway spending, regime change, and other geopolitical factors. The list is long.

These days, however, Brazil pays a notably lower rate on its U.S. dollar denominated debt than Italy does. This was unthinkable only a decade ago, when Brazil was struggling with recession and a history of inflationary devaluation. At the same time, the euro was being introduced as a likely new reserve currency, and Italy was one of the members at its heart. This is yet another example of the "impossible" occurring, and not over a tremendously long time frame. But in trying to examine the possibility of trouble ex-ante in sovereigns, the factors of debt load, budget discipline, rule of law, and the stability of the financial system are all key.

Carmen Reinhart and Kenneth Rogoff have written a wonderful book, *This Time Is Different*,[2] on the subject of sovereign debt dynamics over history. Snapshots of their conclusions, such as that a 90 percent debt to GDP ratio is detrimental to growth, have been widely reported. What's more interesting is the difficulty in measuring credit quality with government bonds. The most widely used statistics are ratios of overall debt to GDP and budget surplus/deficit to GDP, as these measure the amount and direction of a government's debt load relative to its economy's productive capacity. Still, as we'll discuss later in this book, determining the path of future indebtedness is challenging, especially as investors look at longer and longer terms. Brazil in the late 1990s was a tremendous investment, at least for a decade, and investors were paid to take the risk. Italy was not so bad, until recently, but investors were not paid very much to take that risk.

Obviously the current wisdom is that emerging-market economies and governments are in far better shape than many developed-market economies. Given their current debt to GDP statistics, this seems to be the case. In addition, because investors are concerned that such "safe havens" as U.S. Dollar Treasuries and Euro German Bunds are in a more precarious situation, there has been growing interest in emerging markets as a new safe haven investment. When the Federal Reserve or the European Central Bank announce that they are lowering rates (and potentially engaging in a devaluation of their currencies through inflation), it is often the case that emerging-market bonds denominated in local currencies are big winners. Other developed-market economies, like Australia and Canada, with large economic exposures to commodity production, behave in a similar fashion. A few words of caution on this type of investment are in order, however. Remember that the total size of these markets is very small, and the amount of money that has moved here is very large. It's likely a good part of an investment portfolio, but the return on these securities is largely due to the movements of the currency. As a result, if the U.S. dollar moves higher, investors will likely book losses. In many cases the volatility of emerging-market currencies (and even the Australian and Canadian dollars) can be breathtaking, and buyers may be surprised by the losses in what they thought were low-volatility bonds. In addition, because the U.S. dollar has tended to strengthen in periods of global economic uncertainty, these local currency bond positions will lose money when other "risky" assets, such as stocks, lose money. Finally, it's likely that emerging markets will continue to follow a bumpy road on their way to development. Their economies look strong today and debt is low, but as we've seen, that situation can change in a hurry.

Writing in 1992, before the Asian financial crisis, Russia's most recent default, and the current European Sovereign Crisis, Jim Grant wrote:

> *Surveying the foreign-government bond market from the vantage point of the Great Depression, Max Winkler, a financial authority who had repeatedly warned against the excesses of the boom, wrote matter-of-factly: "The history of government borrowing is really the history of government defaults." Winkler's dictum was accurate, if cynical. At intervals throughout the nineteenth and twentieth centuries—in the 1820s, 1882, 1910–14, and the*

1920s, for instance—governments, especially in Latin America, had borrowed and defaulted. It was not surprising that governments would borrow over and over again as opportunity presented itself. What was remarkable was that bankers and bond buyers would pliably lend.[3]

Municipal Bonds

Municipal bonds (munis) are a different animal from taxable securities, and really are a small niche in the context of a larger market. But even munis, with a sizeable portion of market participants being individuals, trade with very large bid-ask spreads on smaller sizes. This is because there is a huge variety of municipal bonds and municipal issuers, such that each individual bond has its own specific characteristics. In order to appropriately invest in municipals, investors must be willing to do significant work around specifics. Municipal bonds reference entities with taxing authority, like states, as well as certain specific projects and even corporations.

The key attraction to municipal bond investment is that the coupons that these bonds pay are often tax exempt at the federal, state, and local levels. California state bonds are tax exempt at the federal level for all investors, and tax exempt at the state level for California residents. For states like New Hampshire, with no income tax, investment in munis is less attractive for state residents. However, New York City bonds are particularly in demand due to their tax exempt status across government levels combined with the high income tax rates in New York State and New York City. When looking at yields and potential return in munis, investors must adjust for the tax rate that they individually must pay and therefore determine the value of the bond for them specifically. Because many entities do not pay income tax (e.g., pension funds, foreign governments), there are fewer kinds of investors in munis, and individual investors play a larger role. Specifically, due to the higher marginal utility of the tax exemption to higher tax bracket individuals, rich people tend to be big buyers of munis. This has led to occasional attacks on the tax exemption of the market.

Yields on tax exempt bonds are often measured as a percentage of U.S. Treasury yields (Treasuries are, again, the benchmark bond). In the past this yield typically ranged from 70 to 100 percent of Treasury yields, with the difference being in part the perception of credit quality of municipal bonds versus Treasuries (driving the percentage higher if buyers were concerned about muni credit quality) and the attractiveness of the tax exemption (driving the percentage lower if investors were trying to shelter income from a higher tax rate). Recent concerns about muni credit quality and the Fed buying of Treasuries driving yields lower has caused that percentage to rise higher across the municipal-bond yield curve. Still, the prospect of higher marginal federal and state income tax rates have kept munis very much in demand.

The Demise of Municipal Bond Insurers

Until recently, the municipal bond market was dominated by bond insurance companies such as MBIA, FGIC, and ACA. These companies held AAA ratings from all ratings agencies and transferred that rating to the municipal bonds they insured. About 50 percent of the market was insured by 2007, and most investors didn't look at the credit differences between bonds, due to the homogeneity provided by the AAA insurance companies. Then again, most investors didn't really look at the credit quality of the AAA insurance companies either. After all, AAA means beyond reproach. Unfortunately, in a story that you've seen before and will see again (in this book and in the marketplace), the muni bond insurance firms turned out to be less creditworthy than they appeared. Their business model more or less depended on diversification. The idea was that very few bonds that they insured would go bankrupt at any given time, and the income from the insurance premiums they received on the entire portfolio would more than cover the small number of defaults. This worked in the world of munis as they had, and continue to have, very few defaults. But the bond insurers entered the market for mortgages and began to insure subprime bonds. The diversification and credit quality in that market was much less than they expected (AAA insurers were fooled by other AAA ratings), and huge numbers of defaults eroded the credit quality of the insurers. Today, those insurance companies are limping along. The upshot for the municipal bond market, however, is that the AAA homogeneity that the insurance companies provided is now gone. Suddenly investors are being forced to dig through esoteric documents to discover what they actually own. While good in the long run (people *should* know what they own), the situation has contributed to the angst in the muni bond market as the insurance companies' value eroded just as muni balance sheets began to see stress. Correlation strikes again.

Types of Munis

In the case of state general obligation bonds (G.O.s), the analysis looks pretty similar to that of a national government bond. At issue is tax revenue and expenditure. Recent stresses in the municipal bond market have come from the deep recession of 2008 and 2009 and a corresponding drop in tax revenue. This closely parallels the situation of many developed-market governments. In addition, large long-term obligations to pensioners represent an off-balance sheet obligation that is worrisome. Still, stresses in the quality of state balance sheets have been largely addressed by state governments through lower spending. This is in part due to the fact that nearly all states have a requirement for a balanced budget. According to an October 2010 report by the National Council of State Legislators, only Vermont lacks some sort of limit on spending.[4] Forty-four states require that the governor submits a balanced budget, 41 states require the legislature to pass a balanced budget, and 38 states forbid the carryover of a deficit. This of course does not prevent a state from having a

significant debt load; debt issuance and the resultant interest cost is considered part of the budget. Still, a balanced
budget requires considerable discipline, especially when times
are tough and revenue is down. Much of the drag on job
recovery in 2010 was due to continued cuts in state and local
government jobs.

Apart from the relatively large state G.O. market, local
governments also issue general obligation bonds, and their
credit quality is a result of their own particular financing
situation, just as with states. But beyond the G.O. market,
municipalities issue bonds referencing specific projects. These
revenue bonds can vary dramatically in quality, in keeping with
the quality of the project or the promised revenue stream.
Though the Jefferson County sewer system provides a recent
counter-example, revenue bonds referencing essential services,
like water and sewer systems, are of very good quality. This is
largely because people tend to pay their sewer bills, for obvious reasons. Other revenue bonds might reference the sales
tax or property tax revenue from a certain area to promote
development. Of course if the reference area is depressed,
that revenue may be insufficient to cover the debt service
of the bonds. Ultimately, the municipal bond market is quite
varied. Default statistics in municipal bonds have been very
low in the past, and even in small-revenue bond issues, bonds
are generally well structured. Even given equivalent ratings,
munis have a great payment history. Still, it would be a mistake
to assume that, just because a market has had a good history,
this history will continue. The small issue sizes of most muni

bonds (there are tens of thousands of issuers in a market that is only $3 trillion in size) mean that liquidity is often poor, and investors should have the attitude that any purchase should be held to maturity to minimize transactions costs. That makes credit quality even more important, and the diversity of issuers means careful analysis is as important here as elsewhere in the bond market.

CORPORATE BONDS

Corporate bonds are also typically fairly simple in structure, with a periodic (usually semiannual) coupon and a principal payment at maturity. Sometimes corporates are callable, meaning that the company has the option to purchase the bond back at a set price (often around par) before maturity. Still, it's a simple obligation. The challenge in corporate bonds comes from the analysis of their credit quality.

Many individual investors have some experience with equity markets, and corporate bonds are the nearest parallel to equities. In addition, some types of corporate bonds have traditionally offered the highest yields in the bond market. As a result, many people are beginning to look at *credit*. Because these bonds reference companies, investors familiar with the stock market should find many of the terms and tools used in the analysis of corporates easy to grasp, but there are very important differences that we'll discuss below.

The obvious, but important, question investors are trying to answer when looking at corporate credit (as with any kind of credit) is the extent to which the company will be both willing and able to pay coupon and principal. Unlike in the sovereign context, the emphasis here is more on ability to pay, as usually the legal system requires a company that can pay to do so. (This is not always the case, as evidenced by the American Airlines bankruptcy in November 2011, where AMR declared with about $4 billion in cash and short-term investments on its balance sheet. American Airlines' unsecured creditors are likely to receive pennies on the dollar in bankruptcy.) Clearly the risk of default is a big part of why you, as the investor, are getting paid more in yield to own a credit than with supposedly credit-risk-free assets, such as U.S. Treasuries. Nevertheless, when times are good and trouble seems to be a long way away, it can be easy to lose sight of the things that can go wrong. I distinctly remember a very well-regarded sell-side credit analyst (whose job, remember, is to look at the risk of default in every investment he analyzes) discussing Enron in 2000. His incredulous statement about the company when queried about the complex financials was, "What are you worried about? What are they going to do, not pay you back?" Though at the time the company was a well-respected high-flier, the answer to that question is always "Yes."

Despite the danger of default, investing in corporate credit can be quite valuable. The annualized total return of the S&P 500 from December 31, 2000 to December 31, 2010 was 1.41 percent. The much more lucrative international markets over that decade were up 3.50 percent (the MSCI EAFE index). Very high quality bonds, as represented by the Barclays Aggregate Index (which is currently about 75 percent government bonds), grew at an annualized 5.80 percent over that time frame. Below investment grade corporate bonds, commonly called *high-yield* or *junk* bonds, are often considered to be akin to equities because of their very high credit risk and higher volatility. In fact, the correlation between high yield and the S&P 500 over this same time frame was .69, which means that high yield moved with equity a little over two-thirds of the time. As a result, you might expect that high yield had returns somewhere between the Barclays Aggregate (high quality bonds) and the S&P 500 (equities). In fact, high yield (as measured by the Barclays U.S. High Yield index) had a total return of 8.88 percent annualized. To give you a sense of what that means in returns, $10,000.00 invested in the S&P would have grown to $11,503.00. $10,000.00 invested in the MSCI EAFE would have grown to $14,106.00 and $10,000.00 invested in the Barclays Aggregate would have grown to $17,573. $10,000.00 invested in high-yield bonds would have grown to $23,414.00, 103.5 percent more than it would have in the S&P 500. Admittedly, the decade was extreme in its returns year-to-year, containing some of the best and worst years in the short history of high yield (or equities), as well as generally declining interest rates (good for all bonds, and unlikely to continue), but nevertheless the returns are interesting.

Still, the return figures above are those of indices, not individual assets. Some stocks in the S&P 500 did very well, and some went to zero. The same is true of credit. It's important to try to find securities that offer an interesting return with less downside risk. This is true across all asset classes, including credit, the rest of the fixed-income universe, and equities. So how do we pick individual credits? After all, buying "the index" is not necessarily going to get you to your investment goals.

Credit Risk and the Portfolio: One Bond and a Bond Portfolio

Let's start with a one-bond portfolio. Imagine you put all of your money into one investment (not a good idea). What would you be concerned with? Income? Sure. Price return? Yes. But with credit you also have to look at two other measures: probability of default and loss given default. What is the likelihood that you won't get your money back, and if that happens, how much money will you lose? In a simplified held-to-maturity, bought-at-par example, your income is going to be determined by your coupon, and your price return will be zero. So the unknowns are really in the downside default case. This brings us to a very important key in fixed-income investment, especially in credit. Investors take "yield" to be their return. However, that is only the best (though the most likely) case. There is also a downside case in which your return is often much less than the promised yield. It is your job in doing credit analysis to determine the likelihood and severity of that downside case and then decide if you're getting paid to take that risk. Unlike equities, there is no upside beyond your yield (in a held-to-maturity example). If the company does really well, you get your yield. Equity investors may get double or triple or more relative to their original investment. If the company does really poorly and goes bankrupt, equity investors will get zero, but bond investors will also lose a bunch of money. So the returns on bonds are asymmetric in that you take the (usually small, but definitely important) risk of a big downside for a limited upside. So your one-bond portfolio will probably be OK, but if it isn't, it's going to be ugly.

In addition to the optionality problem that we'll talk about in a future chapter, this makes diversification within bonds an important concept. A ten-equity portfolio can have half of the holdings go to zero, and, if the other half double, then you're at least back to square one. In a ten-bond portfolio, the likelihood that even one bond goes to zero or defaults with a high loss given default is low. But if it does happen, it will be very difficult for the other bonds to provide enough return to make the portfolio whole. So a credit analyst's job is difficult in that he must determine the likelihood of a very unlikely event that can be catastrophic in its effect on your portfolio. No pressure, though.

The Four Cs

The key to determining the likelihood and severity of default is looking at a company's (or really any borrower's) ability and willingness to pay you back. The basics are the so-called "Four Cs" of Character, Capacity, Collateral, and Conditions.

- *Character:* Management can make debt repayment a focus or can instead take on additional (though legally allowable) risk that makes it more difficult to ultimately pay debt back. A hot high-yield market (like in 2005–2007 or late 2010 into 2011) can allow many borrowers to roll over their debt, but also includes deals designed for private equity sponsors to take money out of the business in the form of dividends. High-grade companies often come to the debt market to raise money to buy back shares. By themselves, these actions can be reasonable, given that the resulting capital structure might be sound. But these actions are often signals of an unfriendly stance toward bondholders. In extreme cases, character also refers to the borrower's honesty. J.P. Morgan once famously said, "The first thing is character. Before money or anything else. Money cannot buy it."[5]
- *Capacity:* A business or a borrower has the capacity to pay its debts based on its cash flow and its current balance sheet. Measures of capacity, which we'll detail later, include debt relative to earnings and interest costs relative to cash flow.
- *Collateral:* Often loans are backed by more than just the borrower's legal obligation. To provide additional

safety, many lenders require some sort of property to which the lender has a specific claim in bankruptcy. Collateral can range from cash or property to equity in a subsidiary. Residential mortgages are a classic example of this.

- *Conditions:* Related to capacity, conditions refers to the economic climate and ability of a borrower to ride out a cycle. Often analysts look at a borrower in the light of current conditions. In good times this can lead to an overestimation of the borrower's ability to pay.

The Four Cs is a useful construction and indeed gets to the idea of willingness (character) and ability (the other three), as well as a framework for a crude analysis. However, I'd like to get into a little bit more depth.

Credit Metrics and How to Think about Them

Many equity investors build complex models of a company's income statement and how it might grow in the future in order to determine what the value of the equity might be in the future. Credit analysts usually start with the balance sheet to determine, not what the company's income might be, but what will be available to pay bondholders. In addition, because the upside of the company is irrelevant (you'll only get your yield, the equity investors get the upside), most credit analysts spend the majority of their time on what could go wrong, versus what could go right. That makes them a gloomy bunch.

The first metric to examine in all companies is the amount of debt that company has in relation to the amount of money it makes. The most commonly used ratio is Total Debt to EBITDA (or Earnings Before Interest, Taxes, Depreciation and Amortization) and is called the *leverage ratio*. EBITDA is the preferred measure of income, because bondholders get paid before the tax man, and depreciation and amortization are noncash items. There is no hard and fast rule to figuring out what an acceptable number is for Debt to EBITDA. In the first place, a high ratio (a highly leveraged company) may be safe, because its business model is very consistent. Regulated utilities often have high leverage ratios because their business is stable and highly regulated. Conversely, a low ratio (a lightly leveraged company) may be dangerous, because the business is highly cyclical and the analyst is looking at the company during a particularly good time. Miners, steel mills, chemical companies, and some energy companies are often in this category. The second reason that there is no hard and fast "best" leverage ratio is that often more levered companies are required to pay investors a higher coupon. While this may be a more risky investment, it is the credit analyst's job to decide what the best risk-to-reward ratio is for a given risk tolerance. Nevertheless, a company's leverage is a very important metric for determining ability to pay, and it is the first place that credit investors go.

The next ratio that dominates credit investment is EBITDA to interest payments, also called the *coverage ratio*.

This measure is pretty straightforward, in that the analyst is trying to determine how much operating income a company has to pay the ongoing debt service. Again, the cyclicality of a company is an important input, as it is important that the company has the ability to make payments throughout the business cycle. In the "Four Cs" framework, the leverage and coverage ratios are some combination of Capacity and Conditions: What are the ratios, and how might they change, given the business model of the company?

An additional and related consideration to the coverage ratio, which only looks at the company's ability to pay interest and debt amortization, is the liquidity of the firm. This can be an immediate consideration if there is a large debt maturity on the horizon, or it can be the longer-term issue of how to make the principal payment of the debt at maturity. Most corporate bonds are structured to have a principal payment at maturity that is equal to the original investment amount; that is, there is no amortization, as only interest payments are made between the initial sale of debt and the maturity of the bond. Most companies depend upon the market to *roll over* or refinance their debt, which can be difficult when that roll-over is supposed to occur during a period of either market or individual company stress. In the darkest days of the most recent financial crisis, the Federal Reserve committed to buying commercial paper, as many firms which depended on this short-term financing (including such blue chips as Johnson & Johnson and John Deere) found that investors had very little desire to buy any debt of any type, no matter how short. As a result, the expected roll-over, even for high quality companies, became difficult. Most companies do not structure themselves to be able to pay off all of their debt upon maturity, which at times of stress means the analyst must understand what sources of cash (from operations, from lines of credit, from asset sales) a company may have. This is best understood and examined before the stress occurs.

When It All Goes Wrong

Sometimes, despite the best analysis possible, the chosen company runs into trouble. Sometimes the analyst takes a risk knowing that there could be trouble, and what seems to be a low probability event comes to pass. Sometimes the analysis just wasn't that good. In any event, if you look at a bunch of credits throughout a cycle or two, you'll end up with some defaults. Knowing that is true, it's important to do some default analysis work on all of the credits, no matter how good (remember Enron, not to mention World-Com, Lehman, Continental Illinois, Texaco, etc.). The most important two questions to answer in default are where you sit as a debtholder and what assets the company has that might help pay you back. The priority of payments in bankruptcy broadly starts with secured creditors, then moves to unsecured creditors, then finally to preferred and common stockholders. Set against that array of claims are the assets (or, if the company is deemed to be more valuable as a going concern, the earnings power of the assets). So before it all goes downhill, the credit analyst needs to see what kinds of assets or earnings power the company may have that would cover the debt claims in a bankruptcy. With regard to earnings power, the leverage ratio is very helpful as a stress-case EBITDA number divided into the current debt amount gives the analyst a pretty good view of what the company would have to be sold out of bankruptcy for in order for each level of debt to get paid back. In this case it is important to remember that, in good times, companies trade for notably higher multiples of EBITDA than in bad times, and companies rarely go bad in very good times.

Away from the leverage ratio, the assets of the company are an important input to what your recovery value might be, or what you're left with after the loss, given default. I recently went through the bankruptcy process with a coal mining company in Australia. Though the journey was painful, ultimately our loss (beyond the foregone interest payments, which certainly matters) was very low, because the assets of the company fetched a very good price as part of the bankruptcy proceedings. In the initial analysis of the company, despite what at the time seemed to be lackluster management (and what turned out to be horrendous management), I got comfort from the asset value. That asset value further gave me confidence to hold the security, despite an unpleasant ride in market prices. The initial investment was a bad decision that was saved (mostly) by the fact that in the analysis I examined what would happen in a default. For all companies, the asset value figure is, in theory, found on the balance sheet in black and white ("Total Assets" is usually in bold), but in reality it is a more complex figure that requires a thorough review of both the footnotes of the financial statements and some general digging around. What usually comes out of that process is not necessarily a precise number, so much as an understanding of the coverage the assets may give. One last note: don't include cash as an asset; companies almost always spend it before you can get your hands on it as a bondholder. Again, in the "Four Cs" terminology, this part of the analysis is all about Collateral.

Credit Ratings as a Framework for Default Probabilities

What's more interesting about the credit rating agencies is that, in an effort to show that their ratings are broadly correct, they have compiled a bunch of information about the probability of default for each rating category. In a 2006 Moody's study, they found that the average cumulative five-year default rate for AAA issuers was .08 percent, and that for single A issuers it was .41 percent. The average cumulative five-year default rate for Ba (equivalent to S&P BB) issuers was 7.86 percent, and the same figure for Caa bonds (equivalent to S&P CCC) was 39.32 percent.[6] So the probability of default is not linear at all. The additional step down in ratings (or, thought of with less regard to the rating agencies, quality) incurs a much greater likelihood of default. According to S&P, the worst year for investment grade defaults from 1981 to 2009 was a tie between 2002 and 2008, with .41 percent.[7] The average default rate for investment-grade issuers over that time frame was .11 percent per year, with nine years having zero defaults. For junk bond issuers the average default rate was 4.37 percent, with the worst year being 1991 (when Drexel Burnham blew up) at 11.04 percent. While the widest yield spreads to risk-free Treasuries in the high-yield market's brief history were recorded in 2008 and 2009, the default rates for those two years were 3.48 percent and 9.23 percent, respectively. We can thank Ben Bernanke, Federal Reserve chairman, for all the liquidity.

Even away from being "wrong" by not purchasing a bond at the lowest price possible, an analyst has a tough job. Take the default statistics above, with the average yearly default of high-grade being .11 percent and the average high-yield default being 4.37 percent. (This doesn't factor in recovery rates on default bonds, so losses are actually less.) Those numbers mean that, in an average year, about one in nine hundred investment-grade credits will default and one in twenty-three high-yield credits will go bad. But the additional income that investors receive for buying those bonds can be in the range of 1 to 3 percent in investment-grade and 3 to 8 percent or more for high yield. So there is definitely incentive to purchase the "right" bond, and a reward for doing just that. Furthermore, timing a cycle to buy bonds when they offer significant yield but the forward default statistics are likely to be low is a key factor to successful credit investing. Still, the analyst, especially the high-grade analyst, is actually trying to precisely and accurately forecast the likelihood of a very unlikely event. That is extremely difficult. Getting back to the asymmetry of bond returns, where you take all the downside risk with very little upside, it's very often (99.89 percent of the time with high-grade bonds) that your investment will get through the year with no default. But if it doesn't, you better make sure you have enough return in the rest of your portfolio to cover it. Then again, trying to increase your return by stretching for more income means increasing your portfolio's default risk!

Credit Default Swaps Market

Credit Default Swaps (CDSs) have been the center of recent concerns in financial markets. Initially designed as a hedging instrument for corporate bonds, the market for these swaps has grown dramatically in size. In 1998 the market size was estimated to be around $300 billion, in 2010 the estimated size of the market was in the hundreds of trillions of dollars. With so much in the way of potential money movement, the market for credit derivatives has taken the blame for market ugliness in 2008 and again in 2011. But these instruments are not too different from the interest-rate derivatives market that has been active for decades. In each case a buyer and a seller engage in a contract (standardized by the International Swaps and Derivatives Association, or ISDA) whereby the buyer pays an agreed upon premium and the seller agrees to provide protection on a certain nominal amount. In effect, the buyer is buying insurance, and the seller is selling that same insurance. The big difference between swaps and insurance is that the buyer of insurance does not need to actually hold a position in the credit, and though the positions are marked to market, there is no underlying principal value. This means that, subject to margin requirements, buyers and sellers of swaps can achieve very high levels of leverage on their positions. Interest rate swaps can cause significant gains and losses, but it is very unusual for interest rates to jump by more than 20 basis points in a day. On the other hand, because CDSs reference corporate credit, the interest rate can change much more dramatically, especially when there is a default. As a result, the participants in the market are potentially highly leveraged to a volatile instrument.

Some market regulators have complained that so-called "naked" CDSs, or CDSs that are not paired with corresponding bond positions, are to blame for market volatility. This is similar to the complaint that companies level against short sellers of their stock. While certainly having the ability to short credit can make a market move down in price more quickly (especially since most corporate bonds are difficult to short, because the holders are concentrated and trading is spotty), it is not the CDS buyer that causes a credit to be fundamentally stressed. More recently, European countries have complained about CDS markets causing higher yields on their borrowing, but subsequent bans on "naked" CDSs have not helped bond prices. Furthermore, the machinations that European regulators have engaged in to keep the Greek default from triggering CDSs was potentially damaging to banks that may have used CDSs as a hedging instrument against the losses that will no doubt flow through to their actual bond positions.

The bigger risk in CDS markets comes from the leverage that the CDS allows. Banks, particularly, will report their CDS exposure on both a gross and a net basis. This means that, while they may have written contracts on a certain gross amount, they have engaged in offsetting contracts to *net out* their positions. Unlike actual bonds, however, there isn't a security that changes hands and thereby leaves a clean balance sheet. The offsetting obligations, unless they are to the same counterparty, remain as exposures to the opposite sides of each trade. This counterparty risk is a major problem, not so much when the CDS itself is triggered by a default, but when the counterparty itself defaults. If a certain bank has exposure to a defaulted counterparty on one side and a solvent one on the other, the bank no longer can expect its positions to net out, as the defaulted counterparty is unlikely to pay on its obligations. Given the trillions of dollars worth of nominal trades and the fact that defaults on the CDS obligations are more likely to lead to higher counterparty risk, this is the root of the market vulnerability.

MORTGAGES AND OTHER ASSET-BACKED SECURITIES

Bonds backed by assets and their attendant cash flows are among the most complex fixed-income instruments available, given the frequent callability of these securities as well as the overactive imagination of structuring banks around the slicing and dicing of cash flows. Happily, because many investors are also asset-backed borrowers (in the form of the mortgages on their houses), it is often the easiest fixed-income asset class to explain.

Residential Mortgages

Mortgages in the U.S. share a common feature that is quite familiar to all homeowners: the ability to prepay. The U.S. housing market would look very different if borrowers were forced to carry their loans to the full term of the original contract. Instead, 30-year loans very rarely reach the full 30-year maturity. In fact, the typical 30-year mortgage lasts a dramatically shorter time period. This is due to a number of factors, not the least of which is the sale of the underlying asset. If you move, you pay off your mortgage (it's in the documents), and this typically pays off the entire loan (unless you're underwater). Another, often more typical, reason for prepayment is a refinance (refi). The dramatically falling interest rate environment of the early to mid–2000s was the setting for a "refi wave" that took out trillions of dollars of mortgage product. In effect, mortgage rates (which typically move with U.S. Treasuries) moved lower and lower, and more and more people took the opportunity to lower their monthly payments. At the same time that the mortgage refi boom lowered monthly payments on a given loan amount, lower rates also allowed a given payment size to enable borrowing a larger total, leading to increased buying power. This was one key factor for a massive increase in debt load for the U.S. consumer.

But for the investor in mortgages, this period was maddening. The callability of mortgage product is good for the borrower, but terrible for the investor. (This is always the way with options and is one of the key concepts in this book.) As rates fell, mortgage investors who had expected to receive a 6 percent yield over a long period of time were suddenly given their principal back. While receiving principal should be the highest goal of a bond investor, the trouble came when investors went to reinvest this par amount. Because rates had fallen, mortgage investors were only able to reinvest at a new, lower yield of, say, 4 percent. This highlights a key risk in all fixed-income instruments: reinvestment risk. Without the callability of the option to prepay, reinvestment risk is more easily measured as the investor's belief in what rates will be when a bond matures. But prepayments add significant uncertainty to the timing of principal. Furthermore, investors don't tend to prepay when mortgage rates rise (unless they move or just want to pay off debt). Instead investors receive that principal back when they'd like to keep the higher interest rate. Conversely, if rates rise, investors who would love to receive principal back more quickly are stuck with a lower rate.

We earlier discussed duration as a measure of the sensitivity of bond prices to interest rates, but as you can imagine, when a bond is callable as mortgages are, this changes the duration of the bond over different interest rate scenarios. If interest rates fall, prepayments become more likely, and the duration of the security (the average amount of time it takes to get your principal back) falls. If rates rise, the duration of the security rises, as borrowers are disinclined to refinance what is a very low interest rate loan. If you recall, this is the opposite of what we'd like as investors. Since bond prices go up more in a falling-rate environment when durations are long, we'd like durations to be long when rates fall. But for mortgages, durations are short when rates fall. So we have less exposure to price upside as rates fall. Bond prices go down more if durations are long when rates rise, so in a rising-rate environment we'd like to have a low duration. But with mortgages, durations go higher in a rising-rate environment. This sort of math is nothing more than restating the fact that the option that borrowers have to prepay at any time is very valuable. We'll talk more about options in bonds later, but suffice to say for now that, when you sell an option, you'd better get paid a notably better yield.

As for market structure, there are two basic types of U.S. mortgages available to a fixed-income investor: agency and nonagency mortgages. Agency mortgages are backed or guaranteed by a Government Sponsored Entity (GSE) like Freddie Mac or Fannie Mae. These companies have the implicit backing of the U.S. Treasury, due to a currently unlimited line of credit that has been drawn to the tune of hundreds of billions of dollars. Even more important, it has become even clearer that the housing market is an important part of the U.S. economy, and these companies exist to make home purchases more affordable. By putting the government's weight behind these mortgage loans, the rates for borrowers decrease.

The solvency of these companies came into question in 2008 as the mortgages they guaranteed began to default at a dramatic rate. Furthermore, these companies also held large portfolios of mortgages. Finally, the equity capital they held relative to their asset base was quite small. In effect, their government backing (and their government mandate to lend more) encouraged the GSEs to allow poor loans with poor collateral. In the end, the U.S. Treasury stepped in and wiped out the value of the common stock and the preferred stock. Still, because these companies hold such an important place in the U.S. mortgage market, the U.S. Treasury felt compelled to support them in *conservatorship* and stand more explicitly behind their loan guarantees.

The market for U.S. Agency mortgages is approximately $9 trillion, and as such represents a significant portion of the investment universe. Because banks are not required to hold significant capital against these loans, they are particularly popular for bank portfolio managers. Leverage is highly available from a number of larger international banks and brokers, as the collateral quality of these particular bonds is considered to be high (basically on par with U.S. Treasuries themselves).

The other type of mortgage security that has come into dramatic prominence lately is the nonagency mortgage (also called a *private label* mortgage). Because these securities lack the backing of a GSE, the investor is not only exposed to prepayment risk, but also to credit risk. In other words, these securities are also callable (prepayable) at any time, but the bigger issue is ability of the borrowers to pay. As a result, investors spend much more time looking at the credit quality of the borrower. Metrics to know include vintage (when the loan was done), loan to value ratio (how much the borrower is taking versus the appraisal), FICO score, and loan structure (whether fixed or floating, 15-year, 30-year, or other). As with agency mortgage bonds, the loans are pooled and sold as a bond. Unlike agency mortgages, the bonds usually are structured to expose investors to various risks of default. This is common practice among many different kinds of asset-backed products, and is also important in understanding the subprime mess.

In general, investors in a nonagency mortgage pool don't want to hold the risk of the entire pool. Instead, various different types of investor want to hold different risks. A risk-averse insurance company may want protection from defaults in the pools, whereas an aggressive hedge fund might want to get more reward from the pool by being more heavily exposed to the credits within the pool. The underwriter of the mortgage does this by tranching the pool into different bonds. A tranche is a slice of risk measured by the percentage of principal loss that the tranche can take. As an example, the "senior" tranche of a high quality mortgage pool might be immune from 20 percent of principal losses in the underlying pool. The more junior slices will be exposed to the principal loss up to 20 percent in order to provide that protection. The 20 percent amount for the senior tranche is called *credit enhancement.* The risk that senior bondholders have is that the 20 percent number is breached. However, even if the 20 percent number fails to be sufficient to protect senior bondholders from *first loss,* they will nevertheless receive all of the remaining principal available. Junior bondholders face a different risk. In addition to the first loss on the bond occurring at a 5 percent loss on the pool of mortgages, junior bondholders are completely wiped out at 20 percent. The prospect of a 100 percent loss on any bond is not often in an investor's mind. This density risk (having all of your risk concentrated in a slice from 5 percent to 20 percent, for example) plays an important, but often underestimated, role in the risk for asset-backed securities, especially given that most tranches are created so that the probability of first loss is very low. In the simplified 100-20-5 percent example shown in Figure 3.1, the underlying collateral (pool of loans) would likely have a very low probability of default in the model, so that the likelihood of first loss

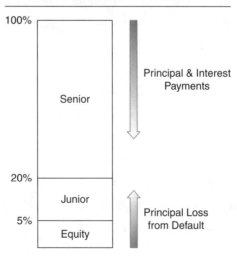

FIGURE 3.1 Tranching risk of an asset pool into various asset backed securities.

on the junior tranche would be 1 percent. This might get an A rating, the senior would get a AAA rating, and the equity tranche would have a very high interest rate to compensate investors for taking a small, but almost certain, loss.

As the underlying mortgages pay down, typically the senior tranches receive that principal and also pay down. As the underlying mortgages default, the realized losses (the difference between what is recovered on the property and the original loan amount) flow up from the bottom. Clearly the lower tranches are riskier, and the higher tranches are less risky. However, it is an analyst's job to determine what the true level of risk is and how well each individual tranche is compensated for that level of risk.

The Subprime Crisis

In 2007, the nonagency mortgage market was beginning to crack. The previous five years had seen explosive growth in the market for *subprime* bonds, generally defined as securities backed by loans to individuals with low credit scores. The twin beliefs in the ability of structured products to define risk and in ever ascending prices of homes allowed for previously unheard of lending practices. Homebuilders, land speculators, mortgage brokers, real estate agents, and buy-to-flip investors participated and drove the U.S. housing market ever higher. The underlying causes of market excitement for real estate are many, including poor equity performance, very low interest rates, and a political enthusiasm for homeownership. But giving low-FICO borrowers money based on nonexistent or often fraudulent data is doomed to failure as nearly as much as is buying large chunks of those same assets. What were people thinking?

Structured products were the flavor of the month in the investment universe, as they offered relatively high yield combined with a high credit rating. Essentially, the market underestimated both the likelihood of the individual borrower to default and overestimated the safety of the structure in which the loans were placed. The typical subprime bond had significant credit enhancement; that is, it had a large portion of equity and junior debt below the senior debt in order to make the senior debt's exposure to loss minimal. Because rating agency models did not include the possibility of a significant downturn in home prices, the corresponding loss given default for each loan was believed to be low. In addition, because of the modeled low likelihood of home price declines, the probably of loss in the first place was low. Finally, the presumption in mortgage lending that geographic diversification would protect lenders led to nationally poor lending practices. In the past, with the exception of the Great Depression, home price declines had been limited to regional economies, such as Texas in the 1980s. It was then believed that real estate was a local phenomenon (location, location, location) and a national home price decline was nearly impossible.

As it turns out, the real estate bubble was not only national, but global. The financial conditions that created a mania for owning homes existed in many countries, including the U.K., Spain, Hong Kong, and Ireland. Other countries, such as Germany and France, were less affected but nevertheless saw notable increases. For subprime, the feedback loop that caused ever increasing prices and ever more aggressive lending ended when there was no one left to buy and the economy began to slow. The models that said that 20 percent credit enhancement was enough were wildly incorrect, both because losses on each default were larger (house prices went down so much that, in 2010, 25 percent of borrowers were underwater), and because so many borrowers had depended on ever increasing prices to be able to afford their financing. In a rising market, when someone can't afford his payments, he can sell his house and reap a gain. In a falling market, that same borrower sends in his keys and walks away, and bondholders take losses. The belief that 20 percent credit enhancement could cover all scenarios is only correct in a world that continues to act according to the model.

What occurred is that the likelihood of loss in the junior tranche moved from small to nearly certain as the models broke down and a coordinated global real estate slowdown made real estate assets much riskier and much more correlated with one another. The risk of loss on the senior tranche moved from vanishingly low to probable. But because of the difference in density, loss experience in each tranche was dramatically different from what rather high ratings of similar tranches would have suggested. In addition, because rating agencies define a default as any loss of principal, senior tranches that took or were forecasted to take any amount of principal loss had their ratings dramatically lowered. This did nothing to defuse the fear and confusion in the market.

Collateralized Debt Obligations (CDOs) used the same tranching technique as mortgage bonds, but took it one step further. Instead of using actual loans as the constituents of the pool, CDOs used the already tranched-up bonds and pooled those. In effect, the risks were nested one in another. In the later stages of the CDO boom, banks even marketed CDO squareds. These securities used other CDOs as constituents of the pool. What a mess.

The reasoning behind all of this slicing and dicing was that the market believed that risk could be dramatically reduced with enough cushion against loss, in this case measured by credit enhancement. The further belief that the risks of each loan or bond were uncorrelated with one another also quieted whatever small concerns most investors had. Of course, as we've discussed, the risk was not uncorrelated, it was much larger than the market imagined, and the credit enhancement that rating agencies and investors assumed was not sufficient.

Commercial Mortgage Backed Securities (CMBSs)

CMBSs share some of the characteristics of mortgage loans, most notably that the collateral is a piece of real estate. Commercial real estate can be a mall, apartment building, office building, or even a warehouse. Crucially, a CMBS is frequently valued relative to the cash flow that the property generates. A capitalization rate, or *cap rate,* is basically the discount rate on the cash flow of the property that allows investors to arrive at a total value of the property (essentially the cap rate is a discount rate for the property cash flows). The commercial mortgage market got very overvalued in the late 1980s (in part due to international monetary flow into U.S. real estate), and banks that loaned against inflated future cash flows or too-low cap rates got into significant trouble in the recession of the early 1990s. Interestingly, in the 2008 recession, CMBSs and commercial property generally suffered badly in the market, in part due to the same sorts of overvaluation mistakes that occurred in the late '80s and early '90s. However, because models of commercial mortgage value included the distinct possibility of a downturn in price, most CMBS structures held up (this despite the fact that the securitization of commercial property in the form of CMBSs didn't really get rolling until the late 1990s). In addition, the valuation of a property on the basis of actual cash flow (even if a too-aggressive assumption of future cash flow increase is part of the pricing) is still part of the equation. Contrast this to residential real estate, where comparable analysis and property value history try to put a value on a nice view or a good school district. CMBSs share the tranche structure common to many kinds of structured products, such as mortgages, and the 2008 recession exposed the same inherent risks in CMBSs as in mortgages. However, commercial real estate has cash flow at its core, rather than some other, more difficult to value, attribute.

Other Asset-Backed Securities

Bonds, being merely contracts, can be structured in any number of different ways, and can reference or require any number of different sources of cash flow. While corporate bonds reference company obligations and mortgages reference required payments on a home loan, bonds have been made of cash flows from car loans, credit card payments, boat loans, airplane loans, and small business loans, among others. Auto loans and credit card payments are the two most common kinds of nonmortgage asset-backed securities (ABSs), which should come as no surprise to anyone who has considered the kinds of debt that any individual is most likely to have. These structures differ from mortgages, because the underlying debt structures are different. As an example, because most people don't pay down their credit card balances, the nearly perpetual nature of a pool of debt means that credit card ABS has to have a structure that rolls debts from one bond to another, and it has a set of provisions that deal with the possibility that new debt can't be sold against the running credit card obligations. With regard to safety, both credit card loans and auto loans held up very well in the 2008 recession. Credit card loans (as most consumers know) have a huge interest rate, and thus the amount of interest paid over and above what is necessary to cover the bond payments is very large, even if defaults are large. Auto loans, which moved significantly lower in price during the depths of 2008 and early 2009, actually held up very well. This is largely because individuals were more likely to mail in the keys to their houses and go rent than to give up their cars and their ability to get to their jobs. Even car loans made to very low-credit-quality buyers held up.

Bonds, again, are interesting because of the variety of different forms and obligations that a bond can represent. The analysis that each different asset class requires is very different, but ultimately the ability and willingness of the borrower to pay back on time is crucial. As we've seen in many asset classes, the risk-to-reward ratio is skewed, due to the structure of many fixed-income instruments, and we'll talk later about how that affects portfolios.

4

OPTIONALITY AND SELLING THE UPSIDE

Success breeds confidence. But who has a right to confidence except the gods? I had a following wind, my last tank of petrol was more than three-quarters full, and the world was as bright to me as if it were a new world, never touched. If I had been wiser, I might have known that such moments are, like innocence, short-lived. My engine began to shudder before I saw the land. It died, it spluttered, it started again and limped along. It coughed and spat black exhaust toward the sea.

—Beryl Markham, *West with the Night*

We've spent some time so far discussing various asset classes and dynamics around fixed income, but I want to try to bring that together coherently around the concept of *optionality*. When people think of everyday options, they think of something that's good. Having two job offers is better than one. Thirty-one flavors is better than five. We want the ability to choose, because even if we like butter pecan, circumstances might change, and we just want flexibility. Financial options aren't really much different from this, despite the complicated formulas that help investors arrive at precise (though not necessarily accurate) valuations. When we look at how financial options work, it's primarily related to the ability of investors to buy or sell at some future date, or not to. In other words, someone who buys an option typically pays a price (the *premium*) to increase her choice in the future. I believe that investing for income often involves giving up a choice in the future—selling an option—in order to get income (premium). Before we get into these specifics, though, let's take a look at how most people think of income.

YIELD IS A TERRIBLE MEASURE OF RETURN

As we briefly discussed at the beginning of the book, most investors who are searching for income from their investments look at one statistic: yield. After all, in the race to your investment goals, you can take a look at what a bond, stock, or fund is supposed yield and reasonably believe that is what it will give you over time, right?

Not necessarily. Let's take the simplest case: a bond. In most cases, if you purchase a bond, you'll get the yield promised to you at purchase. However, you must hold the bond to maturity and hope it does not default. Your return in the interim period between purchase and maturity will most likely be nothing like the promised yield. This is especially true of longer-term securities, whose prices are more sensitive to underlying changes in yield. If the individual bond you purchased does tumble into default, you lose your coupon payments and must endure a significant capital loss. The average recovery value of a corporate bond on default is about 40 percent; you'd receive 40 cents per dollar of face amount invested. Your recovery may be more or less, but it is unlikely it will be high enough to be covered by any sort of coupon or yield, no matter how high that initial promised percentage was.

What makes bond investment for yield even harder is that your upside is basically your yield. With bonds, there is no unlimited upside, as there is with stocks. If you hold a bond to maturity, the most you will receive is the yield promised initially. However, if that bond defaults or otherwise does not pay as expected, then that yield will change (usually for the worse). This asymmetry in bond returns (upside is your promised yield and downside is pennies on the dollar) means that significant diversification is especially important in bond investing, in order to better ensure the safety of your principal; you want to have plenty of entries in the race.

Well then, how about a money market fund? You'll get your yield on that investment, right? Unfortunately, the yield quoted there is an average over some past period. In fact, money market funds are subject to rapidly changing yields available on short-term securities. In an environment where those short-term yields are falling, money market funds are likely to be subject to dwindling returns, though the reverse is also true. Furthermore, though no highly rated money market funds have had enough credit trouble recently to "break the buck," or not return principal, several reputable fund families have chosen to inject funds with capital over the past several years in order to avoid that situation.

A bond or stock fund is an option that promises you a yield, but that yield is really an amalgam of the yields of the holdings of the fund. Just as with the above described pieces, that yield can change and is certainly not a promise. Is there no good answer?

Perhaps an anecdote might help. I recently ran a marathon, not to finish in any great time, but just to do something challenging. I trained for several months, and when the time came to line up at the start I thought I had a pretty good idea how long it would take me to finish. A couple of factors I did not count on, however, were the extreme heat and humidity during the race. About 15 miles into the 26.2 mile slog, I realized that my goal time just wasn't going to happen. In order to stay in the race, not go to the hospital, and come out with a reasonable time, I had to slow down and change my perspective. I ended up doing OK, but only because I understood what was happening and readjusted my expectations in order to finish with an acceptable time.

This readjustment of expectation happens all the time in investing, and in particular with yield-producing securities.

You may think you're getting one yield or return, but suddenly an issuer runs into trouble or the market as a whole hits a rough patch. Even if your portfolio doesn't sustain a default or significant principal loss, you may receive a very different total return from your original yield expectation. Similarly, if you invest at the start in only the highest-yielding securities, expecting to get that yield as a return over a long period, you might as well try to run a marathon at a sprint pace and hold on to the hope that you'll finish at that rate—or at all. Furthermore, as we discuss at length later, investors have a notoriously too-narrow set of expectations about what is possible in the future.

The right approach to investing for income is not simple: you must look at other statistics besides just yield. With bond funds, you get a greatly diversified set of individual bonds. While the yield at purchase of those bonds might be high or low, and the corresponding reported yield on the fund might be high or low, the fund is subject to capital gains and losses, as well as the potential for default, just as individual bonds are. However, with a sufficient time horizon and a diversified portfolio, you are likely to get a reasonable return for a given level of risk. Bonds play an important part in many portfolios, and not just because they provide a source of income. Bond positions also typically have a low correlation with stocks and generally have lower volatility. Though stocks over time have tended to outperform bonds, mixing bonds in with stocks historically has done very little to decrease return while lowering the volatility of that return significantly.

We've seen that yield is a statistic that is computed as a snapshot, but income is something that you receive over a long period of time. The yield your portfolio is running at a moment in time may not be indicative of the income you receive over the course of the race. It is therefore vital that investors see the various factors that might affect their income, including defaults, capital gains, and reinvestment rates. By having a more comprehensive vision of what goes into that check you receive every month or quarter, you'll have a better ability to evaluate which investment might best meet your needs over the long run.

So if yield is not the appropriate measure, how can we evaluate potential investments? I think the best method is to think about investment in fixed income as selling an option. Options, in financial lingo, are the right to buy or sell an asset at some price at some future time. But the concept is much simpler. Really what options represent is both flexibility and leverage to the future, as in more job offers or more ice cream flavors. The opposite of having options is not so much having zero options, however. The opposite of having options is being short options. Being responsible for providing flexibility and leverage to another person in many future outcomes is difficult.

OPTIONS BASICS

Call options are the right to buy, and put options are the right to sell. Basic option theory explains that the value of a call and a put on the same security are related through the value of a stock and the time value of money. What's most important, however, is that options increase in value as volatility increases. As an example: if you hold the option to buy a stock at 30 (the *strike price*) and the stock is currently at 20, you have an *out of the money* call option. "Out of the money" in this case just means that the stock has to move higher in order for the price to be higher than the strike price. If the price is higher than the strike, the option has intrinsic value; in other words, you could exercise the option at that moment and make money. But again, the more interesting question is whether that out-of-the-money option is more valuable if the stock typically moves in a range from 18 to 22, or if it moves in a range from 20 to 40. Of course the call option is more valuable if the stock has more volatility, because the likelihood that the call option will be *in the money* or higher than the strike price is higher.

Some more options basics: a graph of a call option's payout versus the underlying stock is shown in Figure 4.1. The *x* axis is the price of the stock, and the *y* axis is gain or loss. If the investor buys a stock at the strike price, they will gain value as the stock rises one for one. The reverse is also true: if the stock falls in value, the stock investor will obviously lose money. The payout of purchasing the stock is shown by the dashed line. The investor has to put a certain amount of money in, so she only makes money if the stock goes above her initial purchase price.

The call option buyer pays a premium, so his downside is limited to that premium. If the stock goes down, the call option will just expire and that's the end of it. This is attractive both because of the defined downside and because of the leverage that the option investor has. While the stock investor must put down the full value of the stock, the option investor merely pays a premium (usually far less than the value of the stock). To make a profit, option investors need the stock to move enough above the strike price that their premium is also covered (remember that they start in the hole, due to their premium outlay).

Options pricing modeling was pioneered by Robert Merton, Fischer Black, and Myron Scholes. The Black-Scholes model incorporates several variables, including the stock price, the strike price, the price of money (the *risk-free rate*), the dividend rate on the stock, and the stock's volatility. None of these should be too surprising as inputs. Figure 4.1 shows

FIGURE 4.1 Stock and at-the-money call option payouts.

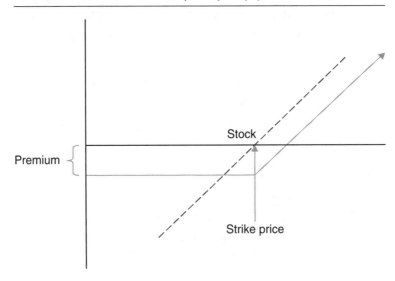

how stock price and strike price matter. We've talked about volatility. The dividend rate matters only because you don't get the dividend when you own the option. And the cost of money is just that: the opportunity cost of having your capital tied up in the option. Don't let the crazy differential equations scare you, this is simple stuff. You want choices, but you have to pay to get them. How much is just what the Black-Scholes equation tells you.

But the Black-Scholes equation is still a model, and as such it relies on a series of assumptions about the world. The most important of these assumptions is that asset returns are normally distributed. A normal distribution is more commonly known as a *bell curve* due to its shape, and normal distribution fairly accurately describes the distribution of a group of people's heights. There are very tall or very short people, but most cluster around the middle. Similarly, Black-Scholes assumes that stock returns can be very high or very low, but those returns cluster around the middle in numbers that can be graphed in a bell shape. Though it turns out those returns do cluster around the middle, the shape is not normally distributed. The difference between the assumption of Black-Scholes and the reality of financial markets is pretty important, because the Black-Scholes option pricing model gets out of whack in crazy markets (this is, of course, when most models get out of whack). We'll talk about this a bit more later, but for now, suffice to say that the simplicity of the Black-Scholes equation gets most, but not all, of the complexity of the value of options. What it does not describe is more accurately discerned qualitatively (with your common sense) rather than quantitatively (with your super-computer).

OPTIONALITY IN FIXED INCOME

Let's try to apply the general concepts of options and optionality to fixed income. Think about the asymmetric payout profile of bonds. We've talked about how it's pretty likely that you're going to get your coupon, but in some cases you could have a big loss. When an investor sells an option, he receives a premium. If the strike price is out of the money, it is pretty likely that the investor will receive that premium and not have any further commitment, because the value of stock never reached the strike price. In fact, the vast majority of options expire worthless. So both in purchasing a bond and in selling an option the investor takes a small risk of a larger loss in order to receive some small payment.

Consider corporate bonds. Say you are the owner of a manufacturing company and you decide to get a loan from the bank to invest in your factory. There is no doubt who the legal owner of the business is. However, if your investment goes bad, the bank is going to get the factory (and perhaps the rest of the assets of your company), not you. So the ownership of that factory is conditional on success.

Now imagine you are the bank. You may not feel as though you own the company, but you have likely specifically structured the loan contract so that you have first claim on the assets of the company if the owner is unable to make payments. We've already seen how priority of payments and claims work in bankruptcy. Bank lenders are typically pretty high up in that priority of payments, meaning that you are "first in line." So instead of thinking about you, the bank, loaning the company money, what if you think about it in terms of options? Imagine that the bank owns the assets of the company, but in addition to that ownership the bank also has sold the upside of those assets to the equity holders. In option terms, the bank has sold a covered call on the equity that it owns. The bank will receive, for selling that call, a premium in the form of the coupon on the loan. The equity owners will receive the upside of the productive capacity of the company and therefore effectively have a call option on the assets. So corporate bonds are really an ownership stake in a company, where the bondholders have sold all of the upside of the company to the stockholders in return for a premium. If things go wrong, you can be sure that the equity holders will get nothing, because their options expired worthless, whereas the corporate bondholders will get something, but certainly less than they had expected to begin with.

Robert Merton, who was instrumental in the formulation of the Black-Scholes model, expressed just this idea, that the value of equity is an option on the productive assets of a company. I've tried to chart this in Figure 4.2. The dark dashed line is the value of the entire enterprise, regardless of which part of the capital structure is claiming ownership. If the bondholder sells a call option to the stockholder, the stockholder's payout is the solid angled line that precisely duplicates the

FIGURE 4.2 Stocks and corporate bonds: bondholders have sold the upside option to stockholders.

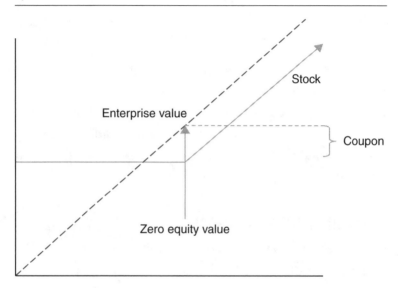

value of a call option. The stockholder will make money if the assets are valuable, but the downside is limited (in this case, to a zero equity value, which may not feel like much limitation). On the other hand, the value to the bondholder is capped on the upside. The value that the bondholder receives to cap that upside is the coupon on the bond, which is directly analogous to an option premium. If things go really badly, the bondholder gets the downside, despite being capped on the upside.

To take a different asset class, MBSs (mortgage-backed securities) are an explicit example of the optionality present in fixed income. When a borrower takes out a mortgage in the U.S., the typical contract states that the borrower can refinance at any time. This means that when a homeowner with a mortgage needs to sell, he can sell his home and use the proceeds to pay off the mortgage debt, or a borrower can refinance that mortgage to a lower rate, even if he has no plans to move. Think about it from the lender's standpoint. If you lend someone money at 6 percent to buy a house, you are expecting to get a 6 percent return (yield) on that note. If rates go to 3 percent, however, the borrower will likely not keep paying that 6 percent mortgage. Instead, he will refinance with a lower 3 percent loan. Conversely, if rates go to 9 percent, the borrower will likely keep the 6 percent loan and count himself lucky to have it.

This works out badly for the lender in both cases. In the first case, the lender is expecting to get 6 percent, and instead, because the borrower has the option to prepay the mortgage, the lender suddenly receives all of its money back. But when the lender goes to reinvest, rates are no longer at 6 percent, but instead have moved to 3 percent, so the return is halved. In the case of rates moving higher, the lender has lent money at a 6 percent rate, and because there is little chance of a borrower paying back the debt early, the borrower is stuck with the 6 percent loan when the new price for similar risk is 9 percent. Think about what happens to the price of the mortgage. On one hand, if rates fall, the lender is likely to get its money back quickly, so the price of the mortgage is not going to move much above par. In addition, because the borrower is likely to get its money back quickly, the duration of the loan decreases dramatically. On the other hand, if rates rise, the lender is unlikely to get its money back very quickly, because the borrower will wait as long as possible to give up that great 6 percent rate in a 9 percent world. As a result, the duration of the bond will be longer and the price will fall fairly quickly. So mortgages rise less in a falling rate environment and fall more in a rising rate one. It's the worst of both worlds for the investor, and the way that the market makes up for this poor option profile is to demand a higher yield from the borrower.

So the optionality in the loan or in the bond (made up of a group of loans) has a dramatic effect on the duration of the bond and therefore also on the change in the bond's price, given different interest rate moves. What's important here, however, is that the change in price is not linear. The investor is short an option and therefore it's almost a "heads I lose, tails you win" situation. The only way that the investor really wins is for prices to stay pretty close to unchanged. In other words, the best situation is one with low volatility.

Mortgages are a pretty clear example of optionality contained within the fixed-income market, because there is an explicit call option that the investor sells with every bond that she buys. The borrower (the homeowner) can call, or buy back, the loan at any time, at par. Thus, by the contract that is the bond, the investor in the bond has sold or shorted that call option. But many other fixed-income instruments have significant optionality (or really, negative optionality), because there are implicit call options that the investor or bond buyer has sold.

Imagine investing in government balance sheets. A government body has a position similar to that of a company's equity holders. They sell debt and use the money on some presumably productive asset. But what claim does the bondholder have if things go wrong? Not much. So it's as if the bondholders have sold a call to the government without any corresponding ownership of the underlying asset. In that sense, government bonds are the riskiest debt, because, as discussed earlier, there is not only the question of ability to pay but also a question of willingness. In a further twist, the government body that the debt references can, at least if they have control over the lending currency, engineer a "soft default" through inflation and money printing, which leads to the devaluation of the real value of the debt while still repaying the nominal principal and interest. Recent government debt that is linked to inflation indices mitigates this problem, but those issues remain a small part of the overall market.

EFFECTS OF OPTIONALITY ON INVESTMENT

Thinking about fixed-income investing as the business of selling options puts a completely different spin on the activity than just chasing yield. We've already seen how options increase in value with volatility. So presumably fixed-income investments do poorly in an environment of high volatility. Indeed that is the case. Bond prices of mortgages that are guaranteed by the government agencies decrease, not only when U.S. Treasuries go down, but also when U.S. Treasuries oscillate wildly. Corporate bond spreads to U.S. Treasuries, a measure of the additional yield investors require to own

corporates versus "risk free" assets, move noticeably higher
when stock volatility moves higher.

Figure 4.3 shows the VIX index versus high-grade corporate bond spreads over the course of the past decade. The VIX
is merely the implied volatility of the S&P 500 from the prices
of traded options. (In a sense, you just run the Black-Scholes
equation, but instead of solving for the value of the option
you solve for the volatility, because the option price is determined by the market.) Certainly there is an argument that the
VIX moves higher when stocks go down, and therefore the
correlation between stock prices and corporate bond spreads
is more relevant. But the spikes in the VIX and the spikes in
corporate bond spreads show markets that do not move in the
same way or with the same psychology as that for stocks.

FIGURE 4.3 Corporate spreads are highly correlated to volatility: It's an option!

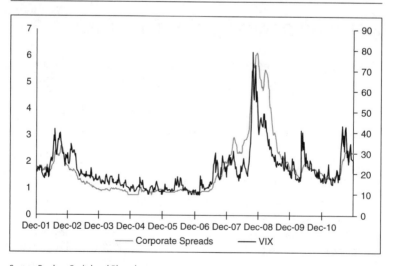

Source: Barclays Capital and Bloomberg

There are several periods of fear and multiple jumps in both volatility and spread that confound models that distribute returns in a bell curve–fashion. Looking at the long period of complacency from the middle of 2003 until the middle of 2007, it is in some way unsurprising that leverage built up in the system and that more and more investors reached further and further for an extra bit of carry. Add to this environment slowly rising U.S. Treasury yields, and it was a time when getting returns from fixed income on the long-only side was very challenging. In addition, the yield curve was flat (as you can see from the December 31, 2006, yield curve graph shown in Figure 2.2). The Fed began raising front-end rates at the beginning of this period, trying to slow the economy. But ten-year rates did not move higher as they usually have. So the carry trade of borrowing short and lending long was also not available to investors in this time frame since, with a flat curve, there was no spread between front-end and long-end rates. So investors engaged more and more in carry trades by borrowing with lower, less risky money and trying to invest that money in riskier securities. This is, of course, a recipe for serious trouble. Bond investors are typically unaware of the risks they are taking until those risks are staring them in the face. So when volatility spikes during market stress periods like the Asian Financial Crisis, the Enron/WorldCom debacle, or the Global Financial Crisis of 2008/2009, corporate bonds react in a very nonlinear way. To put it another way, bond investors look at the value of their coupon payments when times are good, but look to the value of the assets that they're going to receive when times are bad. When the overall value of the asset has a chance to move below the strike price because of volatility spikes, the premium on the covered call suddenly becomes a lot less immediate than the claim on the asset itself.

Bond investors don't invest to lose money. Because yield is such an immediately obvious measure of potential returns, bond investors anchor their expectations on that number. Recently I stood up from my chair on the trading floor and asked my desk what they thought returns on various fixed-income asset classes would be for the coming year. It was natural for the desk, and for all investors, to anchor those expectations on the yields those asset classes were currently providing, for example, "Is high-yield going to earn its coupon this year?" When a particular bond investment goes bad, the yield number starts to slip away in a hurry, as that thought process gets overwhelmed by the likelihood of a permanent price loss.

A great example of this psychology is embedded in the market's reaction to the subprime mortgage market. Investors in those securities were seduced by those bond's AAA ratings and their relatively high yields. Now when I say "high yields," you may think of numbers like 10 percent or 15 percent. But they were only *relatively* high yields. So those bonds sold in the market for a very small spread to some floating index (in this case LIBOR, or the London Interbank Offered Rate, a measure of the rate at which banks lend U.S. dollars to one another over short periods of time in London). Where most AAA bonds were being sold at LIBOR + 0.01 percent or thereabouts, these securities were selling for, say, LIBOR + 0.36 percent. The offer was an extra 35 basis points (bps) of yield per year to buy a bond backed by horrible loans to questionable borrowers. But the rating agencies had blessed these bonds with AAA ratings, and therefore the fixed-income buyer base bought them for the extra 35 bps (remember, in good times only yield matters). To put that in context, for a $1 million position, the extra yield per year is $3,500. Not zero, but not a fortune by any means.

The demand for subprime bonds went up, because of the extra yield that the bonds paid, so even that tiny extra yield went down. At the same time, the difficulties that a subprime borrower might have in paying back the loan were papered over by the tremendous availability of those loans (more about this in a bit). So the market carried on being a terrific place to make an extra three and a half grand on your million bucks, until the dam broke, and suddenly that $3,500 didn't seem like very much. If a bond merely goes down in price by 5 percent from 100 to 95, the investor sustains a $50,000 loss on the $1 million position. So the investor would have to wait for more than 14 years to get her money back in $3,500 increments. Suddenly the panic set in on these huge subprime bond positions, and the yields that investors demanded in order to own them skyrocketed, causing large losses. Investors panicked particularly dramatically because these securities were AAA! No one buys AAA bonds with the expectation that they'll *make* money. Maybe an extra couple grand is nice, and tell me what that yield was again? But when things get ugly, AAA bonds are supposed to pay you back. When the universe of AAA bond investors begins to sustain a loss, you know that you're going to have trouble.

YIELD AS A CUSHION

The one place where a yield measure can have value is as a measure of downside cushion. For most fixed-income instruments, the only protection the investor has against loss is the income return of the bond. There are any number of ways to lose money in bonds and not very many ways to get more than yield. But when prices decline for whatever reason, the total return you receive from bonds can still be reasonable if the yield on the bond is high. This is why corporate bonds that are below investment grade can be safe when yields are high, even if risk is also high. The yield cushion is analogous to the value-stock investor's concept of *margin of safety*. When your yield cushion is LIBOR +36 bps on a subprime bond, not a lot can go wrong. In November of 2008, junk bonds yielded around 22 percent. While a lot did go wrong, that pricing more or less implies that every company will go bankrupt within a few years. At that time, it felt like the end of the world, and I would occasionally opine that if the pricing that was implied by the market wasn't enough of a margin of safety, then the only thing to buy was a gun and a bunch of ammunition. My refrain was, "I don't know how to invest for the end of the world." On one particularly ugly day, my colleague and muni investor Chris Ryon said, "I don't know how to invest for the end of the world ... But I'm learning."

Indeed, purchases made at that point felt terrible, and every bond I bought in September of 2008 was cheaper in October. Every bond I bought in October was cheaper in November. Every buy seemed to be a bad buy and every sell seemed a good sell. Nevertheless, the opposite turned out to be true. I believe that, in mid 2012, U.S. Treasuries offer a similar skewed risk reward, but in the opposite direction. Because there is so little yield available (as of June 12, 2012, the ten-year Treasury yielded 1.60 percent), there is equally little cushion available. Sure, the U.S. could turn out to be more Japanese (with their perennially low yields) than seems possible at this moment. The distribution of possible outcomes is much wider than the market assumes, as usual. But because yield levels can't go much below zero, and inflation is now running above 2 percent, the real return available on Treasuries is terrible. Future returns also seem unlikely to impress. The margin of safety in U.S. Treasuries is low.

NORMAL DISTRIBUTIONS AND OVERCONFIDENCE

Nassim Taleb, in his book *The Black Swan,*[1] spends a great deal of time talking about the problems with normal, "bell curve" distribution assumptions as exist in the Black-Scholes equation. One of his ideas is that, when you assume a normal distribution of returns, you underestimate the probability of extreme events. This is called the "fat tails" problem, in reference to the idea that the actual distribution of outcomes has more occurrences on the ends than the bell curve would indicate. Figure 4.4, which shows a typical bell curve (that takes 30 seconds to reproduce in a spreadsheet), is familiar to anyone who has studied statistics. Johann Carl Friedrich Gauss (1777–1855) was a prolific German mathematician who, among many other accomplishments, brought us the curve illustrated here, which helps to describe distributions around the average of a sample. (He was later commemorated on the ten-Deutschmark note that was removed from circulation on the introduction of the euro.) In the case of the heights of a group of people, the distribution works pretty well. What you'll notice is that most of the observations cluster around the average, and fewer and fewer observations occur as you

FIGURE 4.4 The infamous bell curve: A normal, or Gaussian, distribution.

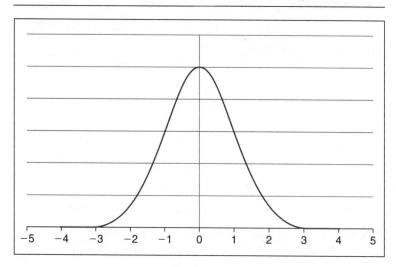

move further away from the average. In fact, as you move only slightly further from the average, the number of observations declines dramatically. The numbers shown on the x axis here are also known as standard deviations. One standard deviation on either side of the average (between -1 and 1 on this graph) contains, in a normally distributed sample, about 68 percent of the total number of observations. Two standard deviations (from -2 to 2 on this graph) contains about 95 percent of the total number of observations. Obviously, finding an event that occurs outside of two standard deviations is very unlikely, as it would only be among about 5 percent of observations.

While human height observations generally fit this kind of distribution pretty well, financial academics and professionals made a pretty large leap when they modeled the returns on assets according to the same distribution. At first glance, there is a pretty good fit with the data, and if your sample set were taken from a relatively calm period in the market, you might even see a terrific fit. After all, there are very few days (or months, or years) where distributions are dramatically positive or negative. We may remember them more vividly, but looking at the data, it's typically the case that small moves up and down predominate over large moves up and down by about the amount that a Gaussian distribution (bell curve) would indicate.

The problem comes, not so much around the calm times, but around the less calm times.

In his study *Black Swans and Market Timing: How Not to Generate Alpha,* Javier Estrada looks at the frequency and magnitude of very large moves and how they affect portfolio returns. Using a hundred and seven years of Dow Jones Industrial Average data, he finds that "The lowest of the [ten] best daily returns (9.19%) is 8.6 standard deviations above the mean. This implies that one return of this magnitude or larger should be observed [in a normal, bell curve return environment] every 250,890,349,457,896,000 trading days, or one every 1,003,561,397,831,590 years. Assuming that the life of planet Earth is around 4.5 billion years, we should then observe one return of this magnitude or larger every 223,014 lives of our planet, and yet 10 such returns were observed in 107 years."[2] Interestingly, he wrote this study in November of 2007. We have since observed another bout of extreme volatility, which is not even included in his sample. Yet if you were a typical risk manager, you would likely have used data going back a decade or so to compute the likelihood of a certain loss and you would have found that a 6 percent loss on a single day had a less than 1 in a trillion chance of occurring. If you were very progressive, you could have used the VIX measure of implied volatility to get your standard deviation measure (this is, in fact, what the VIX is). Still the 22.5 percent loss in one day would be laughably, absurdly, impossible. It would be like the odds of seeing a 12-foot-tall person! But of course it happened. So did major losses in 1990, 1994 (in fixed income), 1998, 2002, and 2008.

Interestingly, some of the same people who pioneered option pricing later became principals in one of the biggest blowups in financial markets history. You've probably heard of Long Term Capital Management (LTCM), and I don't want to rehash the history of the firm (that's been better done by better writers and commentators than me). The important takeaway for the purposes of our discussion is that, by underestimating the probability of extreme outcomes, we are also underestimating volatility. If, as debt investors, we have sold a bunch of options, we will often be anticipating a better world for our investment than might actually exist. Sure, the extremely good outcome will be OK, but we won't actually see that upside. But the extremely bad outcome (like a Lehman Brothers bankruptcy) will be much worse than we thought possible.

When these types of "perfect storm" events occur, two things happen. First, you hear about a bunch of failures of hedge fund investors and the like. The emphasis on short-term returns in the investment industry causes massive pressure to "outperform" over a short period of time. When nothing much is moving and the world looks good, generating returns through a strategy that leverages income is very attractive. As long as nothing moves, you make a bunch of money. This is the classic carry trade. If money is very easy to get (because the economy is good and lending standards are low), investors can take a spread between borrowing costs and their lending returns and lever that up dramatically. Because carry trades and leveraged longs depend on a low volatility environment, when volatility rears its ugly head, people lose their livelihood in a hurry. And usually those failures are spectacular. LTCM is just one example, but an excellent one. By many accounts, because LTCM was such an active player in the markets and investment banks wanted to see what they were doing, those same banks loaned money to LTCM at terms that allowed nearly infinite leverage. While these terms are fantastic, if there is any breakdown in the trade (your model is wrong, the ability to leverage goes away, prices move unexpectedly), you can be wiped out quickly. This same kind of leveraged carry trade breakdown occurred in 2008 to everyone holding subprime CDOs.

The other thing that happens when the market gets ugly is that these same people whose business model has just blown up due to a breakdown in a carry trade talk about how the market had a "perfect storm" and a "six-standard-deviation event" occurred. A six-standard-deviation event has a likelihood of 1 in 506,797,346. The suggestion in all of these commentaries is that the failure was not actually their fault, but it was just some sort of freak occurrence that no one could have foreseen. While the specifics of each occurrence may not be foreseeable, the fact that something might happen to upset the delicate balance of a leveraged portfolio is actually pretty likely, at least according to history. You might think that we would learn from these sorts of blowups. But we don't. Myron Scholes, in August 2011, predicted a "golden age" of financial modeling, given that quantitative analysts had solved problems related to liquidity.[3] Certainly Dr. Scholes, who was one of the principal players in the LTCM blowup, understands the limitations of many of the models that he and others have created. But the idea that these models are perfectible ignores the fact of the human condition: that it is inherently impossible to model.

Another *quant* (short for quantitative analyst), former head of quantitative analysis at Goldman Sachs physicist Emanuel Derman, wrote in his recent memoir *Models. Behaving. Badly:*

> *If you cannot distinguish between God's creations and man's idols, you may mistake your models for laws. Unfortunately, many economists are such people. If you open up the prestigious* Journal of Finance, *many of the papers resemble those in a mathematics journal. Replete with axioms, theorems, and lemmas, they have a degree of rigor that is inversely proportional to their minimal usefulness. The simple models [economists] work with fail to reflect the complex reality of the world around them. That lack of success is not the fault of economists, for people have proved difficult to theorize about. ... But it is the economists' fault that they take their simple models so seriously.[4]*

So the trouble comes, not just from flawed math, but really from flawed psychology. The models, investment strategies, and subsequent blowups are perhaps innate in the way that we all think. In his recent book, *Thinking, Fast and Slow,* Daniel Kahneman (who has a pretty dim view of investment professionals) describes the phenomenon of overconfidence through a study done by a group of Duke University professors surveying CFOs of large corporations. The researchers questioned the CFOs about their best guess on returns for the S&P 500, but more interestingly, about what value they were sure would be too high with 90 percent confidence and what value they were sure would be too low with 90 percent confidence. Though the respondents gave a range where 80 percent of the results should have fallen, and only 20 percent should have been outside (with perfect estimation), in reality 67 percent of the actual results fell outside of the range of the survey participants. So well more than three times as many results were surprises.[5] Because of the prevalence of the normal distribution thought process, the overconfidence in moderate outcomes that Kahneman describes is reinforced by the math. "Fat tails" seem to occur frequently, but both the predominant math and our tendency toward overconfidence seem to keep us, and the market generally, from remembering that. In the context of an asset class like fixed income, where surprises are almost always negative (remember, you've sold the upside for a coupon), these results indicate that markets are often too sanguine about possible negative outcomes.

As an example, in reading a number of outlook pieces to prepare for 2012, I had trouble finding much honest skepticism. One piece had a graph of high-yield bond defaults along with the bank's forecast for the coming two years. Though the graph shows default rates moving dramatically (though obviously somewhat cyclically) from year to year in a range of 1 to 15 percent, the bank's forecast for next year is an extremely narrow range of 2 to 3 percent. Certainly it's possible that the default rate for risky corporate loans could be significantly higher, and any analyst would admit this when pressed. Yet the forecast range is extremely narrow, and therefore return expectations (which will certainly be challenged) are equally narrow.

Crises in fixed-income markets combine the overconfidence blind spot with a second psychological anomaly: loss aversion. Again Kahneman's book speaks to many thought experiments that detail most individuals' aversion to loss. The question "What is the smallest gain that I need to balance an equal chance to lose $100?" gets to a measure of an individual's aversion to loss. Most people center around $200 for a ratio of 2:1, such that the potential gain has to be double the potential loss for people to take the bet.[6] If you extend this reasoning, it's clear that losses are more painful to people than gains are pleasurable. In addition, the frequency of gains or losses is more important than the magnitude. Nassim Taleb describes this phenomenon in his seminal book, *Black Swan*[7] and notes that most people are not psychologically capable of losing money frequently and making it infrequently, even if the net result is very positive. Fixed-income investment fits very well into this model, because it rewards you frequently with small gains (coupons) and infrequently punishes you with a large loss (default). So the psychology of investors is such that they overvalue the small gains (yield), especially in good times when the loss seems unlikely.

It has been fascinating over the last several years (as it certainly is in any fixed-income crisis) to watch these psychological factors at work in the pricing of the market. Market participants are enjoying their small gains and good yields, and are overconfident in their own ability to estimate the chance of a negative outcome. They are certainly overconfident in the likelihood that low volatility will persist. But of course, it does not persist. Volatility spikes, and prices begin to decline. Suddenly the pain of losing money looms very large. The asymmetry of bond returns becomes abundantly clear. The additional extra yield that worked so well when the world was humming along quickly disappears in the markdowns investors are taking on a daily basis. Leveraged investors (banks, insurance companies, hedge funds) who had made money on carry begin to need to post additional capital. And all of this occurs all at once. Does it seem like prices would move up and down smoothly and in a rational or "normally distributed" fashion in this environment?

CORRELATION AND FEEDBACK LOOPS

The above scenario introduces two issues that drive the market dynamics of fixed income (and many other asset classes) in a downturn: correlation and feedback loops. Correlation is a measure of how two assets move at a given time. If assets have a correlation of 1, they will move up at the same time and down at the same time. If their correlation is −1, one will move down when the other moves up, and vice versa. In most market environments, the idiosyncratic (asset specific) characteristics of a certain stock or bond will determine a significant amount of its return. However, in a crisis like that of 2008, the individual stories that might drive return move to the background. Many commentators refer to this as a *risk on/ risk off* environment, where asset classes move only according to whether they represent more risk (stocks, high-yield bonds, copper, the Australian Dollar) or less risk (U.S. Treasuries, the U.S. Dollar). The best term I've heard for this comes from my friend Jared Dillian, editor of *The Daily Dirtnap* newsletter, who calls it "the Blob."[8] The "Blob" moves in one direction, and all the lights flash red, and most people pull out their hair. The "Blob" moves in the other direction, and all the lights flash green, investment banks make a bunch of money, and everyone looks really smart. Don't confuse intelligence and a bull market.

Here is the good news: In these environments significant bargains can be found amongst the rubble of a market meltdown. Because fear is driving market moves, especially in an asset class with asymmetric returns such as fixed income, where investors' psychological anchor of "yield" is dragging badly, correlations move toward 1 (all risk moves down together). But the individual stories still drive the default/no default dynamic, albeit with the additional stress caused by economic trouble. It takes a strong stomach, and the willingness to be wrong, but nevertheless these stressed times present the best opportunities. The dynamic and potential upside of a bond changes dramatically when it is bought at $50 versus par. Suddenly the yield measure is less important and the price appreciation that is available dominates (just as the price depreciation dominates in the mind of the investor who has held the bond from $100 to $50). Distressed debt investing can be particularly lucrative, given the risk aversion in the mandate of most fixed-income investors. That said, it's a very risky business and not particularly appropriate for an individual.

November 2008 is arguably the most extreme example of this sort of environment in the memory of any living investor. While I thought I had a relatively defensive portfolio, prices were declining for every sort of bond that wasn't a U.S. Treasury. At the same time, Treasuries were skyrocketing in value. At one point, 30-year Treasuries were higher on the year by 40 percent, and the average high-yield bond was lower by 40 percent. Looking at the dispersion of fixed-income sectors in 2008 versus equity sectors in 2008, fixed income shows much more variation. While stocks in general moved down much more than most bonds, as correlations increased, stocks moved down together. Bonds, however, due to their differing risk characteristics, moved, in some cases, dramatically apart. A carry trade that took income from the differential of highly rated corporate bonds and Treasuries went south in a hurry. I recall a synthetic CDO (basically, a manufactured bond) that was pitched to me in late 2007 by a large multinational bank. It provided great returns if a specific spread referencing this differential didn't move up more than 40 percent from its current level. The salesman said, honestly, "That spread has never been that high in history." Of course, the history of the particular differential he was referencing was only eight years old. By the beginning of 2008 (not even late 2008!) that particular bond had collapsed as the spread discussed had moved not 40 percent, but 400 percent. Investors who had bought into that structure received zero within a few months. I would guess that their appetite for further risk continued to decline as the rest of their portfolios also moved lower in price as credit markets collapsed.

Large decreases in price happen more often than you might think. 1990, 1994, 1998, 2001, and 2008 all provided very interesting environments for the opportunistic investor. Even in very ugly times, bonds tend to pay you back at maturity. In high-yield corporate bonds, which admittedly don't have a very long history with a great data set, default rates have tended to peak in the mid-teens, which means that about 15 percent of the entire high-yield universe defaulted in one year. But in the worst of times, the compensation for default tends to be much higher than this, especially when you consider that, even in a default, you tend to recover something. Alternatively, the average spread of a high-yield bond in the middle of 2007 at 2.25 percent more than U.S. Treasuries didn't compensate investors for the risk of what occurred the next year. All of this sounds like typical "buy low, sell high" advice, and it's definitely easier said than done. But unlike with stocks, you don't have to sell a bond to someone at a higher price to realize a return. Bonds generally pay you back. Still, it's important never to forget that the path to that payment is unlikely to be a straight line.

Feedback loops are also key drivers of dramatic price moves in any market, but can be particularly jarring in fixed income. We discussed earlier the subprime mortgage dynamic, where increasingly easy financing led to very few defaults. Of course, very few defaults led to increasingly easy financing. This feedback loop continued until the credit quality of the underlying borrower was so poor and the additional capacity to purchase homes at ever higher prices was so low that the market collapsed. A similar issue is occurring at the time of this writing around sovereign debt. Again, while "buy low, sell high" is an annoying platitude, recognizing that the fixed-income market is set up to create volatility can help investors to keep their bearings in a hot and an awful market.

With the advent of the euro, market participants engaged in what was termed a *convergence* trade, where, because of the new currency regime, all involved countries should have roughly the same creditworthiness. As such, weaker countries enjoyed lower borrowing costs. This change in the cost of debt allowed Greece and others to borrow in order to finance their governments at lower and lower rates. Indeed, the temptation to borrow ever greater sums of money seems to have been irresistible. The banking systems of countries across the Eurozone were also regulated in such a way that they had every incentive to buy the new debt. Because banks were (and still are) required to hold zero equity capital against their Eurozone government bond holdings, banks bought plenty of peripheral European debt. After all, though the yields available were higher than those of German bonds, the regulatory regime treated them as the same. They thought: "Better carry and no risk!" Furthermore, because the European currency zone tied the participating economies ever more closely, large French, German, and Spanish banks decided that expansion into these areas was a terrific growth opportunity. So to sum up, governments got cheaper and cheaper money, and banks bought more and more. The only trouble was that the peripheral countries of Europe were not, and are not, as good a credit as Germany. According to Carmen Reinhart and Kenneth Rogoff's excellent book *This Time Is Different*, Greece has been in default for approximately half of its modern history.[9] Is it any surprise that they are not going to pay?

The feedback loop of ever lower costs has been replaced by a second loop of unraveling. It works like this: Peripheral countries are running a large primary deficit (money spent more than money earned before interest costs) and have a difficult demographic situation as it relates to entitlements. With regard to the primary deficit, governments everywhere often spend much more in recessions than they make, due both to the stimulative programs and a sudden shrinkage of GDP. Debt/GDP ratios skyrocket, because the debt numerator is going up while the GDP denominator is going down. Regarding demographics, you may have heard the complaints of Germans about Greek retirement ages. The EU has this problem today, but the U.S. is going to be staring at the same problem in a few decades or less.

At work is a simple equation:

$$\Delta d_t = \left(\frac{r_t - g_t}{1 + g_t} \right) d_{t-1} - pb_t$$

Don't complain that you didn't sign up for a math exam; this is really pretty simple. The equation is for the change in debt/GDP, where d = debt/GDP, r = the prevailing interest rate (nominal), g = the prevailing growth rate, and pb = the primary balance (remember the amount that the government has after all revenues and expenses except interest payments).

The important takeaway here is twofold. First, countries need to be in primary balance to get their debt/GDP ratios under control. At the time of this writing, very few developed market countries are. In addition to significant debt service, the U.S. government is spending much more than it is taking in. Greece had a primary balance in 2010 of −4.9 percent, so even if it didn't have any debts at all, and therefore no interest to pay (or if it defaulted tomorrow and repudiated those debts), it would still have to engage in new borrowing of nearly 5 percent of GDP in order to pay its bills. This problem is also illustrated by the debt ceiling debate mentioned earlier. Effectively, the U.S. needs to get its budget into a surplus or risk further deterioration. In a sense, therefore, the debt ceiling debate, as theatrically ridiculous as it seemed, was a good thing. At least the Congress and the President are actually debating real cuts, including cuts to longer-term costs like Social Security and Medicare/Medicaid.

The second key takeaway to the above equation is that if growth is very slow, or interest rates are very high, or both, it is extremely difficult for any country to get out from under its debt load. Right now in Europe the market is getting nervous about the debt sustainability of many countries, but Italy is one of the big ones on the list. Italy has maintained a debt/GDP ratio above 100 percent for more than a decade, but no one was worried. What's the problem? Italy's growth has been lackluster for some time, and the lack of structural reforms in their labor market or in their economy as a whole have led to a stagnant period of growth. (This problem also exists to a large degree in Portugal and Greece, to a lesser degree in Spain, and is not such a huge problem in Ireland.) The issue at work is a feedback loop whereby markets get worried about a country's debt sustainability, so they raise the required interest rate for it to borrow at. Because growth is hard to come by, especially if the country is in the midst of a recession or debt deleveraging, the interest rate is larger than the growth rate. So the debt load grows. So the market gets *more* worried about debt sustainability. So the interest rate on the debt goes up, so the debt gets larger and less sustainable, and the market gets more worried. Once on this runaway train, it is hard to find the brakes. Indeed, Greece went so far down this path that no amount of austerity that was reasonably possible could save the situation, and the only way out was a massive haircut on current holdings.

These feedback loops are everywhere in finance, and finding them before they run out of control can serve the investor very well. As you can see, because of the dynamics of fixed income, feedback loops can generate some great opportunities and gigantic losses.

EXAMPLES OF ASSET CLASSES AND PRODUCTS THAT ILLUSTRATE OPTIONALITY

Convertible Bonds

A convertible bond is essentially a corporate bond with a call option attached. The bond can be converted into stock (hence the name) if the stock trades above a certain predetermined level. Converts, as they are commonly known, are in theory one of the most interesting kinds of bonds out there, because, instead of having sold the upside of the stock performance to the equity holders in return for a coupon, converts actually retain it (or, more properly, the upside is reattached via the call option). What this means is that convert holders can gain significantly in an upside scenario. Furthermore, converts are protected on the downside versus the equity, because bond-holders have a higher claim in bankruptcy. As a result, on the downside, converts can act like a bond, whereas, on the upside, they can act like a stock. It sounds perfect. Unfortunately there are a few warts. First of all, convertible bond coupons are usually very far below what a regular bond would be on the same name. Effectively you're purchasing back the call option you sold to the equity holders with part of your coupon payment. Second, and more interestingly, the convertible bond market is often dominated by leveraged players like hedge funds. This is because these buyers can buy the convert, short the stock (effectively hedging out the call option), and collect an income stream. Because this strategy can hedge out, not just the call option, but a certain amount of the credit risk of the bond (given that the stock price is correlated to the bond's credit risk), the stream of income that convert arbitrage players receive can be fairly steady. This is bad for long-only buyers, because convert arbitrage buyers (as these people are known) are interested in buying much lower coupon and much lower income bonds, due to their ability to lever up the returns.

However, as we know too well, leveraged players' plans are often upset. In the case of converts, the market through 2007 was dominated by leveraged players to the point where many large convert deals were done and the holders' list of each one consisted of the same few dominant convert arbitrage players' names. In 2008, however, those players' carefully constructed strategies ran up against the problem that leverage was no longer easily available and their models broke down. Because these players had to sell and all owned the same bonds, bond prices moved down dramatically, much more so than the prices for stocks of the same companies (on a relative basis). So convert players were losing their leverage and their hedged trades were going against them. It was a complete mess and more or less crippled the asset class. Converts had to get cheap enough that long-only buyers would consider them, regardless of whatever upside the call option might have. Prices for converts had to move significantly lower to attract real money, but ultimately that occurred and the market recovered. Buyers in the downturn were able to get bonds that were as cheap as "straight" bonds (nonconvertible bonds) but had call options attached. The call option was, literally, free. Ultimately, the returns in 2009 were tremendous as a result.

Thus converts are instructive in two ways. On one hand, as a structure they are theoretically very interesting, due to their ability to participate in upside. The optionality in converts is quite explicit, but unusually in the fixed-income universe, it is in your favor as an investor. On the other hand, because leveraged investors are able to take advantage of the structure as well, and in a way that drives prices higher and yields lower, convertible bond markets are particularly susceptible to swings in price due to the availability of leverage and the overall health of the market. So once again, we've found a fixed-income market that has heightened volatility because of the behavior and incentives of some market participants. Understanding these dynamics is very helpful in generating long-run returns.

Preferred Stock

Preferred stock, or preferreds, are almost the opposite of converts. Preferred stock generally has an unlimited life with no maturity, but is callable at any time (after a certain grace period, usually five years) by the issuer. Many preferreds also have a fixed coupon. So when you purchase a share of preferred stock, you are committing to an infinite obligation and a fixed coupon. If rates fall or the company can fund at a better rate, you get your par back. If rates rise or the company's credit quality falls, what happens? You're stuck in perpetuity with those securities paying a lower than market rate. In a bankruptcy, preferred stock is just that, stock. It ranks in priority of payments only slightly higher than common stock and below any debt security. Given that recovery on unsecured debt averages around 40 percent, you can be sure that recoveries on preferreds are less than that (nearly always zero). Furthermore, the biggest issuers of preferred stocks are financial entities like banks and insurance companies. These issuers nearly always recover zero at almost all levels in bankruptcy, further limiting recovery for people invested far down in the capital structure with preferreds. So for all of this risk, you receive a little more in coupon. It seems to me that this is unlikely to be very attractive in most cases. The time to look at preferreds, like anything, is when they have declined dramatically in price. While this usually means that there are significant and complex issues at hand for the credit, at least you stand a chance of getting an interesting income stream along with tax-advantaged income and some potential for capital appreciation. But preferreds at par too often have a very negatively skewed risk profile.

Annuities

There are many different kinds of annuities, and certainly insurance companies will continue to invent new products to attract different sorts of customers. Ultimately, buying an annuity is buying the risk of a particular insurance company's credit, and I'd prefer, from a credit perspective, not to have a one-security portfolio. While state guaranty schemes can provide protection up to a certain amount, that amount may not cover your full investment. In addition, fixed annuities pay, as the name suggests, a fixed coupon. This can be very ugly in a rising-rate environment, in the same way that investing in long-duration fixed income can lead to losses. At the end of the day, annuity investors are investing in some set of securities to help provide the necessary income, whether that's the credit of the insurance company (cheap funding for them, by the way), or a set of funds or indices. As such, I'd consider a fixed annuity a long-duration bond, while variable annuities have the characteristics of the underlying security or index.

Bank CDs

As long as you're government guaranteed due to being under the FDIC limit, bank CDs are a good alternative to short-term fixed income. CDs are not cash, and usually they have a penalty for early redemption, because the bank is using the CD as committed funding and they don't want to have to sell the assets they've bought to redeem your CD early. But if you go over the FDIC limit, a bank CD suddenly becomes a very concentrated credit bet. While it seems ridiculous today that someone would take a concentrated bet on one particular bank, the not too distant past is replete with stories of yield-hungry investors bragging to their friends about the latest and greatest high-yielding CD they bought. Beware of this recurring. The same investor who would gag at the idea of putting her entire portfolio in one bond may turn around and place her entire savings in one bank or in one bank CD.

Money Market Funds

Though they don't pay anything in yield today, money market funds are an appropriate venue for your short-term investment. Until the U.S. government stepped in during the last recession, money market funds weren't guaranteed and therefore could "break the buck." The very term "break the buck" implies that something has gone horribly wrong, and perhaps for the money-market manager this is true. "Breaking the buck" means that the value of the underlying bonds in a money market fund is less than 99.5 cents on the dollar. However, even if money markets don't break the buck en masse, the fiction of a money market fund that every holding is worth 100 cents on the dollar and that investors should treat money market funds as cash is ridiculous. Money market funds are just very short, very high quality bond funds. The idea that in every situation investors will get back $1.00 for their $1.00 invested is another example of overconfidence in the investment universe. One other significant issue is that money market funds are forced to be unbalanced in their allocation to various types of credit. Rating agencies give their highest short-term rating (a different scale than long-term rating but equating to something like A+ and above on that scale) most often to financial institutions, though this is beginning to change. We've seen that banks and the like are very difficult to analyze and require significant amounts of leverage just to run their business. Much of their leverage comes from depositors and can, in many cases, be supplemented by money-market funds. So, not only is it a question of sufficient ratings, but also a question of sufficient supply. The great irony is that after the 2008–2009 crisis, the increased regulation and scrutiny of money markets has driven them to purchase *more* bank paper. In my short-term investments, I'd prefer the paper of lower rated, but ultimately more stable, industrial businesses. Banks can go out of business literally overnight (though for some reason regulators seem to prefer to push it off to the weekend), whereas the decline in an industrial business tends to be significantly slower, even if it happens more frequently. If I'm purchasing overnight or one-week paper, don't I want to buy the bonds that are less likely to go bad over my investment time horizon? But money market funds can't buy these pieces of paper, because the ratings are more of the BBB+ or A− variety, even if the rating doesn't match the time frame.

But in any event, money market–fund investors are part of the issue. They demand the false security of the $1.00 fiction. If money market funds' net asset value (NAV) floated, investors would see the true volatility of their money, but I think ultimately that would be more comforting (and more realistic) than the black box that the stable NAV allows. Money market funds are another great expression of the idea that an investor's reaction is in proportion to his expectations. In 2008, it was easy to find people more sanguine about their 50 percent losses on international stocks than the potential for a 2 percent loss on their money market funds. I'd be more worried about inflation running at 3 percent and short-end rates at zero (or even negative for very front-end Treasuries), producing right now a loss very similar to what investors were scared of in 2008.

High-Yield, Short-Duration Strategies

This might seem like an oddly niche strategy on which to comment, but these types of funds and investment plans pop up all the time. I'd say the most recent culprits were wiped out in 2008, but more continue to pop up all the time. Before the 2008 meltdown, a number of funds promised a "money market alternative" with higher yields. Whenever you hear the phrase "cash alternative," you're supposed to run screaming in the other direction. When people need cash, they need cash. There is no alternative to cash. From an individual security basis, look no further than auction-rate securities. These investments promised to be liquid and "cash-like," until the underlying liquidity providers decided not to honor the imbedded puts. Investors who believed they could get cash liquidity, but with higher yields, ended up with higher yields but zero liquidity. Parts of this market were still frozen, three years later.

Other Strategies

Other strategies that have employed this kind of sales tactic ("more yield and less risk") include a number of *ultra short* funds that invested in non–money-market-eligible securities. In theory this is a good idea, because any time you have an arbitrary market restriction that restricts a large group of investors to a small pool, fishing outside of that pool is probably a good idea. However, these ultra-short funds didn't actually buy all ultra-short securities. They performed an age-old sleight of hand, which is to substitute interest rate duration for maturity when describing an investment as ultra short. When these funds bought securities that were maturing in 30 years or more but had floating coupons, it's true that they were avoiding the risk that interest rates rose. If that occurred, the security's coupon would rise along with LIBOR. However, while duration nearly always refers to interest rate risk, the same concept can be applied to credit risk. If investors require a larger spread to invest in a certain name, you can be sure that the price of the bond with a low spread to LIBOR will go down. Floating-rate notes don't have interest-rate duration (given that their coupons reset frequently, usually quarterly), but they sure do have spread duration. Ultra-short funds that bought 30-year bank paper found that those securities fell by 30, 40, and 50 percent during 2008. Needless to say, this is not anything like cash.

So-called "floating rate funds" are typically populated with below-investment-grade bank loans that float quarterly. In the same way as the long-term floating rate bank paper example mentioned above, these junk bonds don't have much duration risk, but they do have lots of credit risk. Many investors jumped into these funds in late 2010 and early 2011, as they began to be concerned about rising rates but still wanted yield. Even though this same "more yield, less risk" sales tactic was debunked in 2008, when bank loans declined in value by 40 percent or more, the desire for yield trumped even recent experience. Of course, once again this tactic didn't work. Even the idea that these securities will provide increasing yield in a rising-rate environment is incorrect. Because bank loans are callable at par, it's difficult to get any price appreciation. Furthermore, when economic conditions improve, and interest rates rise, these companies will call their loans and reissue new loans with lower spreads. So even when rates rise, your coupon will not likely change much for the better.

Short-duration, high-yield strategies are fraught with difficulty for a few very clear reasons. We've discussed the way bonds move differently with different duration exposures, where high-duration bonds move more for the same change in rates (whether it be spread changes or interest rate changes). But rates don't always move with the same magnitude. When a company goes bankrupt, all of its bonds recover the same amount, no matter if they were going to be due in one month or 30 years. So as credit quality deteriorates, short durations go from being relatively safe (because they don't move as much for each incremental change in yield), to being toxic (because they have further to fall in price to reach the same bankruptcy dollar price). And yet investors believe that short duration is the same as no risk. Trading desks on Wall Street are staffed this way also: Junior traders end up trading the shorter-term securities, because the capacity in most environments to make or lose money in short-term bonds is much less. But again, when credits fall off a cliff, the short-term holders get hurt the worst. Short-term, fixed income is where the asymmetry of bond returns hurts the most, and given that fixed-income investors are already taking asymmetric risk, why exacerbate it?

So bank loan funds, ultra-short funds, and a new generation of *hedged* fixed-income funds (that tout their lack of duration) are really all the same kind of bet: one that confuses lack of interest rate risk with lack of risk. To put it another way, you can't get more yield without more risk. Don't fall for that pitch.

In this chapter I've tried to detail a mindset around investing in fixed income that can help investors navigate difficult markets. Though option models are flawed, the idea of optionality and choice are central to fixed-income investing, largely because the game is often skewed against you. Still, it's not as though you should give up on fixed income. There are tremendous returns available, and careful analysis on individual bonds as well as a broader sense of an appropriate risk-to-reward balance will put you way ahead of the game. In addition, I hope that the mindset I've detailed here can help you navigate markets when they are volatile, as well as help you measure the true risk that exists when everything seems calm.

5

EQUITIES FOR INCOME

There once was in Westphalia, in the castle of the noble Baron of Thunder-ten-tronckh, a young man whom nature had given a most sweet disposition.

—Voltaire, *Candide*

We've talked at length about bonds and the variety of fixed-income instruments that are used to generate income for a number of different kinds of investors. The trap of negative optionality and asymmetry of returns make the task of finding income in bonds very challenging. But investors often overlook a fairly obvious source of cash flow: equities. U.S.-based income seekers are particularly likely to forget about stocks for income, because dividend yields are so poor in the U.S. compared to those in other countries. But globally, stocks can provide a significant, and more important, growing, source of income.

Certainly fixed income has been in favor for the last few years, and going back further, the returns of this broad asset class (as measured by any number of indices) has overshadowed that of stocks over the last ten years or so. Starting point (valuation) matters, of course, and many equity investors would of course point to the historically awful valuation metrics at the beginning of the century, during the height of the dot-com boom. Fewer would make that same excuse with regard to, say, late 2007, and more recent numbers are also suboptimal for equities. But still, there is a reasonable case to be made that the poor returns for stocks over the last ten years set that asset class up for better go-forward returns.

Still, getting wrapped up in a debate about which asset class, stocks or bonds, is going to perform better over just the next year or so is taking a step toward the trap of the market's obsession with short-run returns. Taking a step back, let's just focus on the income available from these various instruments instead. We've discussed already the phenomenon of compound interest with regard to bonds and how most people don't think about it. Again, 3 percent or 5 percent per year doesn't sound all that interesting. Most regular people have been conditioned for the last several decades to look for 10 percent or more on their money. In fact, the so-called "smart money" thought that, if the stock market didn't work for you after the dot-com blowup, real estate was almost certainly the answer to never-ending wealth creation. But neither growth equities nor the money pit of your McMansion really provided much of a compounding income stream. Most people don't think in terms of longer-term returns, especially in a "what have you done for me lately" world of annual, quarterly, and monthly statements. Investment professionals are also often conditioned to think short term and to try to maximize short-term performance. So an asset class that provides a tortoise-like 3 or 5 or 7 percent doesn't fit in with the mantra. Yet this sort of consistent real return can provide some pretty attractive longer-term answers, as evidenced by the performance of the Barclays Aggregate Bond Index versus many riskier assets over the past five or ten years.

But over the last few years, and continuing into the current moment, fixed income has lost some of its allure. First, bonds tried to be something they are not (see subprime CDOs), caused perhaps by global savings imbalances (former Federal Reserve Chairman Alan Greenspan's "conundrum" of low long-term rates) and also by the never ending, ever unquenchable desire for a few more basis points. These days, the Fed has not only put the cost of borrowing at zero, but has made real returns negative on high-quality fixed income, even with very low inflation.

Quick anecdote: I'm at the barber, and some guy pipes up about paying for a new car. He says, "Debt is like laundry, it never goes away." If this is the attitude we are going to have, then debt investors are going to have to learn the hard lessons of the past few years over and over again.

So what's next? What about stocks, but for income? Even without an inflationary environment (which may come, but may not come for awhile, given a highly indebted global financial system), stocks can provide interesting returns. But don't look at stocks as a quick fix to an underfunded 401(k) or a brokerage statement with a bit too much red. Instead, think about the slow, but steady income stream that is available in equities too, and which, right now, is better than bonds. As an added bonus, the tax treatment on dividend income is certainly superior to the treatment on bond income. But even without that advantage, dividend-paying stocks are very interesting as an asset class.

UPSIDE OPTIONALITY AND VOLATILITY

We've spent a bunch of space in the previous chapter talking about looking at the asymmetry of bond returns and the downside of selling options to get income. There's a reason why bond investors are gloomy and stock investors are optimistic. Stocks have a very enviable advantage over bonds in that they have exposure to upside. If, as a bond investor, you've sold the upside to a stockholder, there must be an upside for the stockholder. If you can't beat 'em, join 'em. This is the least appreciated reason to hold stocks for income, because most investors look at income and capital appreciation as mutually exclusive. Dividend-paying stocks, as we'll see, can provide both. In addition, the difficulty with stocks is that they are volatile instruments. But as we've seen, volatility does not just mean to the downside (even though that's when everyone focuses on it). Volatility and unexpected returns can also be an upside. An investment in a stock is, in fact, counting on upside volatility. As long as valuation is attractive (another story and piece of analysis altogether), owning stocks for income can help balance an investor's portfolio.

DIVIDENDS VERSUS BOND YIELDS

I'm not one of those who believe that, because equities are yielding more than bonds, they are obviously and automatically a better deal. In fact, for almost the entire first half of the twentieth century, investors demanded more income from stocks than bonds to justify holding a riskier asset class. It was only with sustained economic growth that investors began to believe that bonds were low-return assets that had to have significantly more income than stocks in order to be worth holding. Volatility is an important part of an investor's experience, but it is too often ignored when times are good. After all, people don't care about volatility when it's volatility to the upside. So, now that stocks have shown their bad side for a decade or so and a generation of investors is underwater, I suspect that those same investors will require significant income in the form of dividend return to be excited about holding riskier assets like stocks. Add the massive intervention and distortion of fixed-income markets that we've seen in developed markets globally, due to central bank buying, and the argument that stocks are "cheap," because their dividend yield is higher than U.S. Treasury yields, is a little skewed.

Probably we'll be in a situation where investors require greater current cash flow from their riskier securities for awhile. But away from the yield statistic alone, that compounding return I mentioned earlier is a big deal. The $\wedge$ in your spreadsheet and the y^x on your calculator are really pretty important over long periods of time, which is exactly the period of time that you want to be thinking about in this business. Yes, dividend-paying stocks, that supposedly bond-like portion of the equity market that really hasn't been a market darling in some time (though that may be changing), is an interesting source of compounding returns. Over any reasonable length of time dividend returns dramatically improve total returns. In fact, dividend-paying stocks have outperformed others over time.

DIVIDEND PAYERS OUTPERFORM

Let's examine how and why dividend-paying stocks outperform others. Most investors think of dividend-paying stocks as a boring part of the market. The moniker of "widows and orphans stocks" has been attached to dividend payers as investments appropriate for those who don't want volatility and are happy with a slow, steady return. Of course, most investors are actually in this category (increasingly so), but most people think that one has to give up growth and total return to get an income return. Table 5.1 shows a few different broad indices' return from both price and income over a couple of decades, compared with a subindex that focuses on dividends. As you can see, the income return of the dividend-focused subindex is higher than that of the broader index. That's the easy part. The total return is also higher, but that might just be due to the dividend payment. But look at the price returns. The dividend subindex outperforms on a price basis alone, relative to the broader index.

The choice that many investors feel they are making between dividend-paying stocks for income and nondividend

ABLE 5.2 Earnings Grow Faster at Companies with Higher Payouts

Starting Payout Quartile	Average Subsequent Ten-Year EPS Growth		
	Worst (%)	Average (%)	Best (%)
One (lowest payout)	−3.4	−0.4	3.2
Two	−2.4	1.3	5.7
Three	−1.1	2.7	6.6
Four (highest payout)	0.6	4.2	11.0

other company pays out nothing and reinvests the full $100 back into the business. Which company should grow its earnings faster: the company that reinvests only $50 or the one that reinvests the full $100? Of course the obvious answer is that the company that reinvests twice as much should grow earnings faster over time. However, this research shows that the opposite is the case. Companies that pay out more to shareholders actually grow their earnings faster over time. Subsequent studies into this phenomenon have shown that it is robust across geographies.

So the outperformance by dividend-paying stocks is not just due to their income properties, but due to the growth of earnings as well. While these findings are initially counterintuitive, I can tell you that companies that pay out cash to shareholders tend to be fairly focused on long-term cash generation, a good thing if you're a shareholder. Private equity bankers who buy public companies with massive leverage in LBO (leveraged buyout) transactions will make a similar

TABLE 5.1 Breakdown of Returns of Dividend-Focused In
Broader Comparable Indices

	Price (%)	Income (%
DJ Dividend Select Index	8.3	4.4
DJ Total Stock Market Index	7.8	2.0
MSCI World High Dividend Yield Index	6.7	4.0
MSCI World Index	5.7	2.3
MSCI EAFE High Dividend Yield Index	7.5	4.3
MSCI EAFE Index	4.6	2.6

Source: MSCI and Dow Jones Index data via Bloomberg. Dow Jones Dividend Select comp
to June 2011. MSCI World High Dividend Index comparison from June 1995 to June 2011. N
comparison from June 1995 to June 2011

payers for total return is not a real choice. In
payers have a better total return (this is a lin
certainly, but definitely contains a good sampl
market environments. Longer-term studies of
divided by payout ratio show similar results.

In delving into the returns of dividend p
nondividend payers, a number of researchers hav
dividend-paying stocks actually grow their ear
than nondividend payers. Table 5.2 summarizes
an Arnott and Asness study from 2003 that com
earnings growth of stocks divided by dividend pa

To put this in plain English, imagine two
both of which make $100 in earnings. One cor
out $50 to shareholders and reinvests the remaini

argument. They would say that a huge interest burden on a company will focus the management team on cash generation, because the interest costs are a cash flow that must be met. Dividends, while not contractually guaranteed, serve the same purpose, in my opinion.

GO GLOBAL

Investors who are looking for dividends are well served by searching internationally, as opposed to just in the U.S. In the U.S. we still have a belief (maybe changing) that CEOs can actually allocate capital effectively and that if companies don't pay any money back to shareholders their organic growth is that much higher. Internationally there is a continued faith in the power of cash returns. See Figure 5.1. It's a well-placed faith, as we've seen. The dividend-paying culture of companies is evidenced by their higher yields and higher payout ratios.

It used to be that Japan had a lower dividend yield than the U.S., partly as a result of their low yields and partly a consequence of their notoriously poor record of rewarding minority shareholders. However, now even Japan has a higher yield and payout ratio than the U.S. International investors seem to have the reasonable notion that the cash they earn from their investments is important. Perhaps their belief in their ability to sell to another investor at a higher price is less due to lower liquidity or a less developed capital market. Maybe there are more family-owned concerns, or companies that have dividend-hungry governments as shareholders. In any event,

FIGURE 5.1 Go Global: Yields and Dividend Payout Ratios Across Geographies.

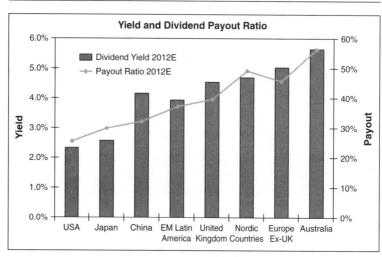

Source: MSCI Indices sourced via Bloomberg as of 9/30/2011.

an income-oriented investor needs to make sure that she is looking at global markets.

A global investment focus can pay off, not just in higher dividend yields and good geographic diversification, but also in good sector diversification. In the United States, the dividend sector is skewed toward telecom, utilities, and financials. (The focus on financials was much more evident before 2008, when those stocks overshadowed dividend payers and the market in general.) But an examination of other markets shows good income opportunities in sectors that disdain dividends in the U.S. As an example, as of September 2011, the Information Technology sector paid 1.1 percent in the United States, but 4.3 percent in both Scandinavia and Australia.

IT'S NOT YIELD, IT'S GROWTH

The secret weapon in the dividend investor's arsenal is not yield, however. The key attribute to successful investment is growth over time. Merely searching for companies that pay a high dividend is likely to have the same result as buying corporate bonds that promise big yields. Investors in both cases are likely to end up with the riskiest securities and therefore are probably going to have a weak total return and fail to receive the promised income stream. Financial stocks in 2008 are a good example of this. Many banks were listed as having high dividend yields in late 2008, because they had a previous record of paying good cash and their share prices had declined dramatically. However, those banks felt the need to retain cash (and still do, more than three years later) and so cut their dividends. The high yield was illusory in this case.

To avoid this fate, investors need to search for growth in dividends. Again, the tradeoff between growth and income is not a real choice. Investors can have both. More important, a long-term investor can reap a much higher income stream from a growing investment than one that pays a high, but fixed, yield. Indeed, this is a major advantage that stocks have over bonds as an income investment.

Table 5.3 details the dividend payment history of the S&P 500 from 1970 to 2010. As we've seen, the S&P 500 is not a great dividend-paying index, but that just makes the analysis more interesting. In 1970, the price of the S&P 500

TABLE 5.3 Dividend Progress for the S&P 500 Since 1970

	Dividends per Share	Yield on Cost		Dividends per Share	Yield on Cost
1970	3.14	3.41%	1991	11.94	12.97%
1971	3.07	3.33%	1992	12.37	13.44%
1972	3.15	3.42%	1993	12.63	13.72%
1973	3.38	3.67%	1994	13.17	14.31%
1974	3.60	3.91%	1995	13.82	15.01%
1975	3.68	4.00%	1996	14.91	16.20%
1976	4.05	4.40%	1997	15.52	16.86%
1977	4.67	5.07%	1998	16.19	17.59%
1978	5.07	5.51%	1999	16.69	18.13%
1979	5.65	6.14%	2000	16.28	17.35%
1980	6.16	6.69%	2001	15.74	17.10%
1981	6.63	7.20%	2002	16.07	17.46%
1982	6.87	7.46%	2003	17.38	18.84%
1983	7.09	7.70%	2004	22.52	24.44%
1984	7.53	8.18%	2005	22.10	24.11%
1985	7.90	8.58%	2006	24.87	27.03%
1986	8.28	8.99%	2007	27.72	30.11%
1987	8.81	9.43%	2008	28.39	30.84%
1988	9.73	10.41%	2009	22.41	24.34%
1989	11.05	12.00%	2010	22.73	24.69%
1990	11.44	12.43%	2011	26.43	28.71%

Source: Bloomberg and Factset

index was slightly below 100. Thus, the $3.14 dividend payout equated at the time to a yield of 3.14 percent. Now imagine you bought a share at that cost and held it throughout the next four decades. The value of your share increased, and that was a source of great returns over that time frame (even if the decade of the 2000s was not a great contributor). But if you focus only on the dividend coming from the index, there is a clear, if occasionally rocky, progression over time. By 1980, your dividend per share of the S&P 500 index had increased by almost 100 percent to $6.16. By 1990, it had almost doubled again, to $11.44. The subsequent two decades saw slower growth, in large part due to the mania for growth stocks (that didn't pay cash and, no surprise given the preceding information, didn't grow). Furthermore, the recession of 2008 took a big chunk out of the dividend of the index as it moved from $28.39 in 2008 to $22.41 in 2009. Still, by 2010 the S&P 500 paid $22.73. If you had held that share from 1970 to 2010, your yield on your initial cost would have been 24.69%. Certainly four decades is a very long time horizon. But the power of dividend growth is a key part of getting income from stocks.

The growing income from dividends in your stock portfolio can also help to assuage your doubt when prices fall. This is another reason to search more for growing dividends and less for high dividends. When recession hits, dividend cuts are less likely from a company with a dividend you expect to grow than from a company that you expect to barely earn its payout.

WINDSTREAM VERSUS CHINA MOBILE: HIGH YIELD VERSUS GROWING YIELD

Many investors screen the market when looking for income using a filter that requires a particular dividend yield. What that often misses is the growth in income that the S&P 500 itself evidenced over the past 40 years. As an example, let's look at two stocks as they stood at the end of 2011 and as they performed and paid over the previous five years. In one corner is Windstream (WIN), a domestic U.S telecom company that is effectively treading water. They are losing land lines as their customer base slowly, but surely, transitions to mobile phone use. The twisted copper pair is dying a slow death. To counteract this decline in revenue, Windstream is signing up broadband customers, with some success. Because their coverage area is generally fairly rural, the broadband that Windstream offers is often the only option for their customers. At the end of 2006, Windstream's share price was $14.22. They had just paid, over the course of the previous 12 months, $1.22 per share. As a result, their yield was 8.58 percent. This was very attractive relative to bond yields at the time, and certainly yield-hungry investors were very attracted to the stock. Fast forward to the end of 2011, five years later. The share price as of December 29, 2011, was $11.85. The previous 12 months the stock had paid $1.00. The yield, as a result, was 8.44 percent. So over the course of a five-year holding period, the stock had returned −16.67 percent, but because it paid fairly consistent dividends over that time frame, the total return was 28.41 percent. The S&P 500 over the same time frame returned −.82 percent, and the MSCI EAFE Index (International Stocks) returned −20.30 percent. So ultimately, despite the "melting ice cube" business of the wireline business and the declining dividend and declining stock price, Windstream stock was a pretty good performer. Still, you started with an 8.58 percent yield. If you didn't touch your stock and didn't care where it went, but were merely concerned with the yield on your original $14.22 cost, your yield in 2011 actually declined to 7.02 percent. This is not terrible and, relative to a number of fixed-income options, it still looks attractive. Nevertheless, your yield on your original cost declined.

Now consider China Mobile (941 HK), a Chinese mobile-phone company that has more subscribers than the U.S. has people. Though China Mobile has struggled with a number of difficult problems, most notably a regulator that has been looking to undermine the company's dominant market position, the company has actually grown its dividend over the last five years, though from a low level. Revenue growth has been strong, as has subscriber growth. This is in direct contrast to WIN. At the end of 2006, China Mobile was trading at HKD67. It had paid, over the course of the year, two regular dividends plus a special cash dividend that together added up to HKD1.28. As a result, China Mobile's yield at the end of 2006 was a relatively paltry 1.91 percent. Fast forward to 2011, where as of December 29, 2011, the stock is trading at HKD75. Over the course of the past 12 months, China Mobile has paid two dividends (no special this year) totaling HKD3.177. This is dividend growth from 2006 of almost

20 percent per year. The current yield is still low relative to WIN, at 4.24 percent, but your yield on your original cost is becoming even more competitive, at 4.74 percent. Your total return is slightly better than WIN, but much better than the S&P 500 or the MSCI EAFE, at 31.35 percent. But the total return is not the point here. Both stocks did very well on a relative basis. Windstream's high yield ended up being fairly attractive and was a wonderful cushion against adverse events (including the general decline in WIN's stock price). But China Mobile's dividends per share actually increased significantly, more than doubling in five years. What originally looked like a poor-yielding asset turned into a much more interesting one. It may be difficult for China Mobile to sustain 20 percent dividend growth per year for another five years, but continued growth should be a larger part of their future than at WIN.

This is not meant to be an exercise in stock picking, and I don't wish to recommend any particular security given the quickly changing nature of the market. This is merely meant to illustrate that dividend growth is at least as important a part of the landscape in investing for income in stocks as dividend yield. Once again, the "yield" number is not only insufficient as a measure, but even can be misleading.

INCOME FROM STOCKS ... FOR THE LONG RUN

Think about the kinds of problems a growing income stream can solve that a static one would struggle with. We've already discussed the possibility of an inflationary environment sometime over the next five to ten years. If an investor has locked in low rates for a long period of time in the form of fixed income, dramatic inflation would be a disaster in terms of maintenance of purchasing power. While stocks did not do very well as an inflation hedge in the late 1970s, they were better than bonds. Even if a company's earnings growth does not match inflation, if that same company grows its dividend in keeping with its earnings, investors are likely to be in a better position than with a fixed income in an inflationary environment.

I've tried to detail here the use of stocks for income, given that I believe most investors think they are giving up growth for income when they make a choice to purchase dividend-paying stocks. The evidence says that isn't true, and there seems to be very little reason to ignore the long-term total return record of dividend payers. Nevertheless, dividend-paying stocks are still stocks, and they can have significant volatility (which can be good or bad). The last serious market downturn, in 2008, showed that, over shorter periods of time, dividend payers can have a significant downside. The worst performing sector in 2008 was financials, to no one's surprise. The second worst performing sector was telecom, a group of companies that broadly performed very similarly to market expectations previous to the downturn. So the companies grew their businesses and their dividends, but the stocks still went down. Given the growing demand for income, it's possible, and even likely, that dividend stocks will get overvalued at some point and disappoint the inevitable late adopters. But longer term, I believe in the capital discipline that a dividend forces on managements, and I think that alone is a powerful tailwind to performance and income generation.

The persistent myth that dividend-paying stocks trade out growth to get income is a fantastic anomaly that investors should take advantage of (while it's still there). It seems that investors consistently underestimate the growth available from dividend payers, or more likely, persistently overestimate the growth available from nondividend payers. Markets are fascinated with growth and all of the darlings of the U.S. market try to project the image of growing to the sky. Interestingly, many of those same companies build up huge, unproductive, cash hordes. What's the point of generating cash if you never return it to shareholders? The best-case scenario is that the company manages to invest it in the business appropriately. But history shows us that the more likely scenario is that the company wastes it on unproductive projects. Companies don't grow to the sky, but investors seem to continually hope that they've found one that will. As a result, they both ignore and create the fact that higher earnings growth actually comes from companies that pay out a portion of their cash flow to shareholders. Furthermore, investors again ignore the compounding return of the income stream of the dividend. In this case it's just like a bond: The income available from stocks is not immediately obvious over the short term and therefore doesn't get computed. Remember the quotes about the S&P 500 return over the course of 2011, when the reported return was flat, while adding in the dividend put the return of the index above 2 percent for the year. This sort of thing happens all the time and when aggregated and compounded, can be very additive to performance. Last, after putting up with all the downside and the limited upside available in fixed income, the prospect of some exposure to upside in your portfolio of income-producing securities is likely a good thing. The market's need for income is likely to extend beyond just a few years. Demographics are inexorable and the fixed-income returns are likely to be challenged, given the current starting point. Take a look at stocks.

6

BANKS: A CASE STUDY

Banks and bankers are by nature blind. They have not seen what was coming. A sound banker, alas! is not one who foresees danger and avoids it, but one who, when he is ruined, is ruined in a conventional and orthodox way, along with his fellows, so that no one can really blame him.

—John Maynard Keynes, "The Consequences to the Banks of the Collapse of Money Values," 1931.

Banks have gone from the darlings of the investment universe to the goats. Of course, this is frequently the road that darlings travel: We build up our idols in order to tear them down. But financial institutions generally, and large, international banks in particular, are currently being vilified for any number of reasons. Looking at a bank's business model is relevant to income-seeking investors for several reasons. Banks represent a potential investment opportunity. At times they have represented a large portion of the dividend-paying stock universe. In addition, financial institutions remain the single largest sector of corporate issuance, especially for investors who are required to buy highly rated bonds. Banks also are large investors in fixed income themselves. More subtly, the incentives of banks and the way that they invest their deposits speaks to the pitfalls of income-oriented investment. Banks are the mechanism for the transmission of financial panic, and also the main targets of that same panic. Let's dig a little deeper.

THE MECHANICS OF A BANK BALANCE SHEET

The typical bank balance sheet has, like that for any business, assets and liabilities. For a bank, though, its assets are basically other people's liabilities. A bank might have some cash, but most of its assets consist of loans. Those loans are the same types of loans that are available to the fixed-income investor: loans to governments, corporations, and individuals. In fact, banks are large participants in fixed-income markets as purchasers. On the other side of the ledger, a bank's liabilities principally consist of loans that the bank has received from other people. The most common kind of liabilities for a bank is deposits, although banks have often been large issuers of short-term bonds. And here is the problem: Bank customers can remove their deposits at any time. However, a bank's assets are not nearly as short-lived. The duration of the deposits is effectively zero, whereas the duration of the loans on the asset side of the balance sheet might be one, two, five, or ten years. As a result, banks typically earn more money when yield curves are steep (in other words, when the difference between yields available on longer-duration securities and very-short-duration securities is very large). The difference between what banks make on their loans and what they pay out on their liabilities is called their net interest margin (NIM). The difference between the value of the bank's assets and its liabilities is the bank's equity capital, or book value.

Equity capital, to any company, is the value of the company over and above the value of its liabilities. But banks don't have much in the way of hard assets, like factories or inventories, as a typical industrial business might. If the value of a factory declines, an industrial business doesn't much care, as long as it can meet its liabilities with cash flow. The interest that banks earn from their loans is analogous to that cash flow, but as we've seen, a bank is funded very differently from most kinds of businesses. Recent regulatory changes and market psychology have forced banks to increase their equity capital as a percentage of the total balance sheet from a high single-digit number (like 7 or 8 percent) to a low double-digit number (like 12 or 13 percent). The idea behind this shift is that this additional equity can provide a better buffer against loss. But even at 12 percent equity capital, a bank is much more highly leveraged than a typical industrial business. To give you an idea of how much more, a 12 percent equity capital base means, obviously, that the remaining 88 percent is debt capital. Most industrial businesses are fairly highly levered if 50 percent of their capital is debt. The presumption is that a bank's assets are of a much higher quality, and are much more able to be valued than a factory or a warehouse full of widgets. But recent events have shown that's not always the case. In fact banks have complained that actually marking the value of their assets is detrimental to their business, because markets jump to the conclusion that they are unable to meet their obligations if their assets are smaller than their liabilities. It strikes me that investors would generally be better served to know more about businesses in which they might invest, rather than less.

BANKS AS INVESTORS

A panic exposes the essence of banking as no lecture, book, or diagram can do. The essential truth about the ordinary bank is that it is no safe-deposit box. Every dollar of the depositors' money is not in storage on the premises all the time. The art of banking is always to balance the risk of a run with the reward of a profit. The tantalizing factor in the equation is that riskier borrowers pay higher interest rates. Ultimate safety—a strongbox full of currency—would avail the banker nothing. Maximum risk—a portfolio of loans to prospective bankrupts at usurious interest rates— would invite disaster. A good banker safely and profitably treads the middle ground.[1]

Relevant to our discussion around investing for income, another way to think of a bank is that it is a massively leveraged investor in fixed income. If the equity component of a bank balance sheet is only 8, 10, or even 15 percent, the bank is borrowing the rest and making the difference. But clearly the bank has to engage in lending that is riskier than depositors presume the bank is in aggregate. As James Grant suggests in the above passage, if banks are too risk averse they won't make any money. Yet banks are supposed to be staid, safe places for money. As John Kenneth Galbraith further suggests, even bank buildings are designed to suggest this safety:

> Money is, to most people, a serious thing. They expect financial architecture to reflect this quality—to be somber and serious, never light or frivolous. The same, it may be added, is true of bankers. Doctors, though life itself is in their hands, may be amusing. A funny banker is inconceivable.[2]

So on one hand, we have this extremely leveraged entity that has a notable mismatch in risk (either from a maturity standpoint or from a credit standpoint, but likely both). On the other hand we have this safe, steady institution where we are comfortable putting our life savings. Which is the truth?

Really, both are correct, but in my opinion, the structure of a bank makes it prone to trouble. With the asymmetric return of fixed income (mostly good income, but with occasional spectacular blowups), how can a bank survive with high leverage? The equity cushion is perhaps sufficient, if depositors take a long view and allow a bank to recover from its loan losses. But depositors themselves have very little upside. To be fair, banks have other sources of income that don't rely on their loan books. Fees for everything are very much in vogue, given that these fees come without leverage or risk. But away from this fee income, banks, to be profitable, are reliant on a high net interest income, lots of leverage, or most often, both. Like any fixed-income investor with a short-term time horizon (remember banks are pressured to show quarterly earnings), in good times they get overconfident in their ability to predict all possible outcomes, both good and bad. It's no surprise that bank risk managers are the most ardent supporters of a very quantitative approach to risk management. Before the latest crisis, banks were constantly examined for their Value at Risk (VaR). VaR is essentially a measure of the maximum amount a bank could lose with 95 percent confidence. In other words, if you look at a bell curve (there it is again!), what is the amount of money that a bank could lose with approximately a 2 standard deviation event? This methodology assumes, once again, that losses and gains are normally distributed. In addition, in plugging in a figure for volatility, bank risk managers used a backward-looking, observable number, weighting most recent observations more heavily. Of course, in the middle part of the 2000s, volatility was very low. If you plug a low volatility number into your risk model, for a given amount of risk your VaR is going to be smaller than if you plug in a high volatility number.

But we've already seen that volatility can cluster and that returns on most of the bank's portfolio are going to be pretty asymmetric in a negative direction. This doesn't even take into account the fact that returns are not, in fact, normally distributed, as we've seen. Not surprisingly, the VaR numbers that bank risk managers reported vastly understated the actual losses they sustained in 2008 and 2009. And it's not the first time this has occurred. Though banks are supposed to be safe, they are very frequently the locus of panic and loss when recessions hit.

It's no wonder that governments step in both ex-ante and ex-post to prop up banks. The FDIC exists to guarantee bank deposits, so that a run on a bank is forestalled due to confidence that the U.S. government will make depositors whole. When that isn't enough, governments tend to step in and either restructure banks or force them to sell themselves to other banks. Often equity holders are the big losers in these transactions, and occasionally bondholders also take losses. However, regulators are reluctant to impose large losses on bondholders, given that it's the bondholders (along with the depositors) that provide the high leverage on which the banking system relies.

This is one reason why the Lehman Brothers bankruptcy was such a disaster. The idea that the Federal Reserve and the U.S. Treasury were going to prop up the financial system, no matter what, was reinforced by their treatment of Bear Stearns in March of 2008. Markets tend to push on the weak point of a situation and constantly test for feedback loops, and after Bear was sold to J.P. Morgan at a great loss to BSC stockholders, the market, after a pause, turned to the next weakest member. Lehman, because it was not a depository bank, could not borrow from the Fed. Though Goldman Sachs and Morgan Stanley quickly became depositors so they could access Fed liquidity in September of 2008, for Lehman it was too late. The market lost confidence in their ability to fund their balance sheet, and the entire leveraged entity collapsed. Merrill Lynch would have suffered the same fate had it not been bought by Bank of America.

The depository banks, joined by Goldman and Morgan Stanley, were propped up by the Fed lending in another example of a government's willingness to support its banking system on an ex-post basis. It is the financial system governments really try to support, not just a single bank. The interconnectedness of banks with one another is equaled only by the interconnectedness of bank health and lending with the health of the overall economy. There is no doubt in my mind that Citigroup, Bank of America, and any other reasonably sized bank in 2008 had, at market values for their assets, a negative equity value. But regulators gave them space, additional equity (TARP), guaranteed borrowing (TGLP), and any number of other acronymed support plans, so that they did not have to engage in a fire sale of their assets. But this leads to the question of liquidity versus solvency. If a bank is unable to come up with money today, but will eventually make good on its obligations, it is illiquid. If a bank will not ever be able, on its own, to make good on its obligations, it's insolvent. The line between the two is very gray, especially in the fog of a financial panic.

LIQUIDITY AND SOLVENCY

> *A bank may be said to be solvent when its assets are so constituted that a liquidation would necessarily result at least in complete satisfaction of all of its creditors. Liquidity is that condition of the bank's assets which will enable it to meet all its liabilities, not merely in full, but also in time, that is, without being obliged to ask for anything in the nature of a moratorium from its creditors. ... If the bank is in immediate need of large sums of money, it can procure them only by disposing of its assets; when the panic-stricken public is clamoring at its counters for the redemption of notes or the repayment of deposits, a bill that has still thirty days to run is of no more use to it than a mortgage which is irredeemable for just as many years. At such moments the most that can matter is the greater or lesser negotiability of the assets.[3]*

Ludwig von Mises had the immediate experience of bank runs in the Great Depression. Recognizing the symptoms of a liquidity crunch is simple only once it has begun. In early September 2008, the Dow Jones Industrial Average and the S&P 500 were solidly in *bear market* territory, down more than 20 percent from their highs. The Nikkei average was down over 5 percent in one day's trading. Investors bought bonds with both hands, as they fled to the safety of high-quality assets. The *New York Times* ran a "hindsight-is-20-20" story about one smart or lucky individual headed out to a Paris vacation. He heeded the evidently obvious signs of market meltdown within subprime mortgages while the rest of the (conveniently stupid) market participants failed to see the writing on the wall and are now nervously awaiting pink slips. But that meltdown was sparked by, though not completely attributable to, the dreaded subprime mortgage sector. Subprime mortgage lending was merely the most obviously underperforming asset class in a series of highly leveraged and increasingly complex transactions that seemed to all have gone wrong at once, causing a global panic in debt markets.

In reality, the assets underlying these transactions had not all gone wrong at once. Though subprime mortgage delinquencies have indeed skyrocketed, other kinds of lending, such as that to corporate borrowers, remained, for awhile, on fairly good footing. However, if no one is willing to buy loans or bonds under any circumstances, the credit markets stop working. The *negotiability* of which von Mises speaks above has also become *liquidity* (of the market) in our parlance, and in that sense refers also to a degree of depth within the now-dominant capital markets model, where a run on the bank morphs into a run on the market's depth. That market depth was tested severely, to the point that central banks across the world injected short-term funding into the banking system in order to maintain orderly lending. It suddenly became clear to market participants that global financial markets require an enormous degree of funding, just to run mundane operations on a day to day basis.

A sea change had occurred in the attitude toward leverage and so-called "structured products." Much of the growth in financial markets over the previous several years, particularly within fixed income, could be attributed to a shifting of and repartitioning of risk. In the past, banks were the major repositories of risk. In particular, they would originate and hold credit risk in the form of loans (both residential and corporate) and fund these loans through short-term deposits. The "run on the bank" that von Mises describes occurred when those short-term deposits were suddenly in demand and the bank was unable to monetize its longer-term loans. With the advent of new financial technology and burgeoning global capital markets, banks and others (including mortgage lenders) were able to originate risk, but then remove it from their balance sheets. The risk was further partitioned to appeal to a large variety of potential investors by dividing it (with the help of rating agencies) into a series of ratable pools. The AAA investor got AAA risk, the BBB investor got BBB risk, and the equity investor got equity risk, all at supposedly higher returns than comparably rated securities with less complexity, as we've seen.

So banks supposedly removed risk from their balance sheets and distributed it to a wide array of investors, effectively diversifying the risk into a large liquid-capital market. Market participants trumpeted this shifting of risk to investors as healthy, but it is becoming evident that there are two inherent problems with the model. The first problem comes in the form of the age-old "run on the bank." This time, however, the lending institution could be a leveraged hedge fund instead of an old-time bank. The hedge fund, in effect, has short-term deposits (its investors, which may be able to remove their money at any time), but holds longer-term illiquid securities. So part of the investor base in risky securities has the same funding issues that banks in the 1930s did, even though the humming supercomputers in the trading rooms and fast cars in the parking lots may indicate otherwise. These participants have been termed *shadow banks,* because they help to fund, through the purchase of securitized pools of assets, lending that used to stay on the balance sheet of a bank. But the term *shadow bank* also refers to the lack of visibility of the leverage that these entities carry.

The second problem comes from the fact that this process of shifting risk separates the origination function from the risk-taking function. When banks lent to a corporation or individual and held that risk, that bank's credit committee had the burden of significant analysis. If however, that same bank merely lends the money to the corporation, but then sells the loan to a group of investors, it has much less inherent interest in making a good loan. Add an additional layer of structure and complexity through the division of risk described above, and the end investors have much less ability or inclination to analyze the risk they may hold. Even if the end investor is a supposedly responsible buyer, the layers of risk and complexity, as well as the inherent distance from the loan origination, make understanding the risk of any given security very difficult. Investors as diverse as highly rated insurance companies,

European and Asian banks, and highly regarded mutual fund families all seem to have taken the plunge.

But banks, in their pursuit of profits and high returns on equity in the good times, decided to get in on the party that they were throwing for their customers. While they touted a "risk distribution" model, in reality they were distributing risk back to themselves, or not getting rid of it at all. Bankers who were paid an annual bonus found that those bonuses went up when they generated more income, and because the risk seemed to be very distant, the cost of capital to purchase or retain investments on their balance sheets was nearly zero. Lehman Brothers owned vast tracts of desert land as part of a development scheme. To purchase that and other risky investments, they and many other market participants leveraged their balance sheets up, so that their equity cushions were as low as 3 percent.

While driven by fundamental weakness in U.S. real estate, in particular subprime loans, the current liquidity crisis became a general lack of confidence in banking and financial institutions globally. If the large international investment bank BNP Paribas proclaims one week that their subprime exposure is "negligible," but then the next week discloses that it is blocking redemptions from several funds that invest in mortgages, because they cannot appropriately value the securities within the fund, what are investors to believe? In 2001, WorldCom and Enron showed us one set of books, then swapped that set for another, uglier set. The financial markets extrapolated at that time that all companies were corrupt and punished them by discounting their equity 50 percent or more in those cases. The Sarbanes-Oxley legislation was enacted. Today, we are continually presented with revised European sovereign budgets that bear no resemblance to the previous, iron-clad plan. Summit after summit of European finance ministers produces a number of vague plans, but the problem is one that can't be solved with a convenient headline.

Banks rely on confidence. With high leverage (even if it is lower today in the U.S.), they are always in a precarious situation, yet bankers, like all market participants, have a profit motive, and like many people, a short investment time horizon. The "trader's option" is a very real example. Risk takers within a bank have incentive to put on the biggest trades possible. If it works, their bonus at the end of the year is huge. If it doesn't work, they get fired. But amazingly, since this is the way of the financial world, they'll likely get hired at another bank. In fact, it seems as though some of the most spectacular losers are the most quickly snapped up.

So when confidence dries up due to opaque bank losses, lending of all kinds stops. Banks won't lend to good businesses, and they won't lend to each other. These institutions do not or cannot continue with their businesses. If the market no longer believes that these financial institutions hold assets that have significant value, then money flows will slow or stop. The severe funding issues in money markets in Europe as well as the dramatic appreciation in U.S. Treasury bills are a symptom of this. When panic takes hold of credit markets generally, financial institutions no longer lend (for example, by providing mortgages). This slows economic activity and creates a recession where none may have existed before or exacerbates an already weak economic backdrop.

THE GOVERNMENT STEPS IN

This lack of confidence becoming a credit crunch becoming a recession is the real risk, and the problem that the Federal Reserve was able to ameliorate with its significant lending programs. Because the Fed controls the money supply, there was and is plenty of money, but no one has the confidence to lend it.

Walter Bagehot, in his seminal work, *Lombard Street*, described the function of a central bank as follows:

> *And with the Bank of England, as with other banks in the same case, these advances, if they are to be made at all, should be made so as, if possible, to obtain the object for which they are made. The end is to stay the panic; and the advances should, if possible, stay the panic. And for this purpose there are two rules. First. That these loans should only be made at a very high rate of interest. ... Secondly. That at this rate these advances should be made on all good banking securities, and as largely as the public ask for them.*[4]

With the structure of the global banking system, governments will always be considered the lenders of last resort. The most interesting thing about the current crisis in Europe is that it is the government itself that is being called into question. This situation points to another vulnerability in banks, especially European banks, that underlines the potentially precarious position of fixed-income investors.

FROM SUBPRIMES TO SOVEREIGNS: BANKS IN EUROPE VERSUS BANKS IN THE U.S.

When you think about the asymmetric returns of bonds, based on the idea that you've sold the upside, it's fairly easy to imagine situations where bond investors can get in over their heads. The old market saying goes, "To err is equities, but to really screw up takes fixed income." While on the face of it, bonds seem to be more staid and less volatile than stocks, the idea that investors (and all people) are more confident about the future than they should be gets them into particular trouble in fixed income. If your upside is small and your downside, while unlikely, is large, you can be sure that in good times investors will ignore the downside to a degree that comes back to haunt them later on.

This problem shows up in some structural differences between European and U.S. banks and is a particularly important issue at the time of this writing (May 2012). We've already discussed what book equity is for a bank and the current trend toward requiring larger equity cushions against potential loss. But the question of how much is enough depends not only on the percentage amount of equity capital (the regulator's focus), but also on what the assets are. While Lehman Brothers may still have failed with 3 percent equity capital if it held extraordinarily safe assets, the fact that it had risky, illiquid real estate on its balance sheet didn't help. More recently, MF Global failed, not so much because of high leverage, but because of huge bets on Italian sovereign debt. It's pretty obvious that, if a bank holds a bunch of very risky loans, capital should be higher. If a bank holds very safe loans, capital could be lower. In fact, this doctrine is behind the Basel regime of bank capital that is being adopted in Europe and which is, to a certain extent, being mirrored by the U.S. Insurance companies (also leveraged-bond portfolios, to a certain degree), which have a similar set of regulations.

In general, U.S. banks have over time tended to hold riskier loans, but with more capital. On the other hand, European banks have tended to hold less risky loans, but with less capital. In theory those two actions are equivalent. But if you think about the overconfidence that people tend to have about the future, you can start to differentiate between these two strategies. On one hand, U.S. banks (again, broadly: certainly Lehman didn't follow this strategy) look at their holdings as risky. There is an assumption of a certain number of defaults and the drivers of risk are often clear. Leveraged buyout (LBO) loans have a bunch of risk, and so banks expect a significant return and hold (at least when regulated properly) a good amount of capital in bad and good times against that risk. European banks, on the other hand, tend to look at their holdings as less risky, or even riskless. The current sovereign debt crisis is a case in point. Banks believed that the debts of various Eurozone countries were beyond reproach, given their membership in the club. European banks were also large buyers of subprime bonds in the years leading up to that sector's demise. Rating agencies certainly helped along both crises by continuing to rate flawed securities with AAA or very high ratings.

But it's a question of overconfidence. If you believe that your holdings are risk free, it makes sense to leverage them as much as possible to get a return. It is easy to build models that show that those holdings are risk free, especially since most models don't take into account a sufficient data set. In 2007 data sets on housing markets showed a fairly robust set of possible outcomes, so bonds exposed to housing prices looked great. If housing markets had continued to be as buoyant as in the mid-2000s, much of the subsequent problems in the U.S. and European banking systems would have been avoided. But of course that didn't occur.

As investors that have some of the same incentives, we can learn from all of these events. In addition, because banks represent a large part of the investable universe for both equity and fixed income, having a handle on their sources of risk is crucial. In a crisis it feels as though analyzing bank risk is akin to analyzing the willingness of the government to prop up a particular bank or the financial system as a whole. Obviously one of the particular characteristics of the European sovereign crisis is that the health of the banking system and the health of the sovereign credit are inextricably linked. Intesa San Paulo

is a bank with relatively conservative opera
a multiple of their equity capital is currentl
government bonds, the bank's operations
conservative. The fact that banks are encou
holdings of sovereign debt is not unique
U.S., banks continue to buy U.S. Treasurie
borrow against those holdings at extraor
U.S. investors can excoriate European ban
much Spanish, Greek, or Italian debt, but t
ture in the U.S. is identical. We can only b
follow the European banking model of p
risky assets have no risk.

It's the same lesson: Thinking about fi
ments, with their asymmetric return an
as risk free no matter how good the under
is a recipe for disaster. Time and time a
good times imagine only positive outcome
mildly negative ones) and get caught in a c
that they thought was impossible. The fact
be structured to be exposed to these sorts o
a surprise, because of recent experience as
banking panics and crises.

7

TOWARD A SUSTAINABLE PORTFOLIO

We've seen that investing for income is a challenging task, not just because investors have to juggle a bewildering array of different economic and credit-specific facts, but also because the market seems to be set up to add volatility and uncertainty over time. While understanding that buying fixed income is like selling an option, and that equities can provide an excellent balance to that asymmetry of return, putting these ideas to work in a portfolio is a different matter altogether. The ideal portfolio is one that provides an interesting income stream, but does not blow up at the first sign of trouble. Frankly, Jim Grant's description of a good banker as one who "safely and profitably treads the middle ground"[1] between risk and reward also accurately describes the best income investors (though I wouldn't want the leverage and liquidity constraints). Some guideposts to understanding when and how to take risk at the portfolio level might help. After all, it's easy to say "buy low and sell high," but, of course, difficult to do it.

MINKSY'S FINANCIAL INSTABILITY HYPOTHESIS

Most conventional economic models assume that individuals are rational and that systems tend to seek an equilibrium condition. Anyone who has sat through an economics lecture has seen curves move on a board (or now, on a computer screen) to simulate an exogenous change in conditions that is then incorporated by the system. The conditions of supply and demand leading to an equilibrium price is a perfect example. If supply goes down, prices will seek a new higher level to match the new supply level with a corresponding new level of demand (presuming there is less demand at a higher price). Hyman Minksy (1919–1996) proposed the Financial Instability Hypothesis, whereby debt accumulation in the financial system *by itself* caused a breakdown in the system. This was a dramatic departure from economic orthodoxy, because it held that economic systems were expressly not seeking an equilibrium point:

> *The financial instability hypothesis has both empirical and theoretical aspects. The readily observed empirical aspect is that, from time to time, capitalist economies exhibit inflations and debt deflations which seem to have the potential to spin out of control. In such processes the economic system's reactions to a movement of the economy amplify the movement— inflation feeds upon inflation and debt-deflation feeds upon debt-deflation. Government interventions aimed to contain the deterioration seem to have been inept in some of the historical crises. These*

historical episodes are evidence supporting the view that the economy does not always conform to the classic precepts of [Adam] Smith and [Marie-Esprit-Leon] Walras: they implied that the economy can be best understood by assuming that it is constantly an equilibrium seeking and sustaining system.

Over periods of prolonged prosperity, the economy transits from financial relations that make for a stable system to financial relations that make for an unstable system. The [Financial Instability Hypothesis] holds that business cycles of history are compounded out of (a) the internal dynamics of capitalist economies, and (b) the system of interventions and regulations that are designed to keep the economy operating within reasonable bounds.[2]

Minsky's characterization of debt markets included three stages: hedge finance, speculative finance, and Ponzi finance. In the first state, the cash flows from projects tend to pay for themselves. You can think of this as an amortizing bond, like a well underwritten residential mortgage. The borrower has the capacity to make the payments, and no further funding or refinancing is necessary to pay off the loan. Speculative finance comes into play when the borrower does not have the capacity to pay off all principal with cash flow, but can only make interest payments. In the residential mortgage example, this is like the borrower who can make the payments on an interest-only loan, but who needs to refinance when a balloon payment comes due.

One key point: In the current financial structure, banks are perpetually in this state. Whereas high-quality industrial companies often can generate the cash flows required to make the principal payment at the maturity of a bond, banks are, by their nature, constantly rolling over their debts. The return on equity of a bank requires significant leverage, and, as we've seen, the mismatch in duration of assets and liabilities means that debt needs to be constantly rolled rather than paid off. Certainly a bank with well underwritten loans may, in theory, be able to sell its assets to the market to make payments (the bank is solvent, but not liquid), and banks at the moment are selling assets for the very purpose of reducing overall debt. But banks are both the enabler of and the product of speculative finance.

The final Minsky finance state is Ponzi finance, in which borrowers cannot pay off either the principal or the interest with current cash flows. In the residential mortgage world this would be analogous to the most recent subprime loans that allowed the borrower in the short term to have a low, teaser rate to afford the house. If that rate went up, the borrower could no longer afford the house and needed to have a jump in income or sell the house. The assumption with these loans, of course, was that if any borrower got in trouble (which could happen by only paying the introductory rate!), he could sell the house and pay off the loan. This only works in a stable environment for house prices, of course. A credit analyst I once worked with euphemistically called deals with this Ponzi characteristic *projections deals,* because you needed to project positive cash flows into the future to make the math work. Needless to say, these deals occur only in hot markets and are the most prone to failure. Nearly every LBO loan is a projections deal, and an active LBO market is a sure sign of a growing Ponzi finance environment.

Minsky's characterization brings together two important points of analysis for the income investor that we've spent significant time analyzing thus far: the individual condition of the borrower and the broader economic system. First, bottom up analysis: what are the individual characteristics of the investment? Is it a hedge finance investment with sufficient cash flows to meet both interest and principal, or is it a Ponzi deal that requires additional financing? Second, top down analysis: what is now and what will be the condition of the financial markets that may or may not promote financial gain or, if necessary, refinance?

BOTTOM UP: MARGIN OF SAFETY

For an analyst of an income-producing security, risk comes in the form of her analysis and a general understanding of the likelihood that she is wrong. Reward comes in the form of a high promised income stream. Value equity investors often speak of a *margin of safety* or the size of the discount to fair value that they are buying a particular stock. That idea incorporates the possibility of missing important aspects of the investment or the "unknown unknowns" that inevitably exist in any situation. With credit analysis, your margin of safety, your cushion against adverse events, comes from your income stream. This does not mean that you are "safe" if a bond has a high yield, in fact often quite the opposite. However, with more income, an investor, especially an investor with a reasonably diverse portfolio, can be wrong more often. Greater yields (and potential returns) come with more risk of default and more price volatility, but that shouldn't be a surprise. There are no free lunches. At the same time, buying a supposedly safe bond because it has a high credit rating, but then not doing your homework, is an invitation to disaster. You may not be taking a big risk if the bond is truly high quality, but how do you know? On the other side of the ledger, a truly horrible company's bonds can be a great investment. The distressed debt community makes its living on these situations. If a bond is trading well below the value of the assets that back it, even a lengthy default proceeding can be profitable. As seasoned bond investors say, "There are no bad bonds, just bad prices."

Examining securities for any length of time means confronting the limits of your analysis. It is impossible to be right all of the time, and the important thing is to know that you will be wrong and decide what your tolerance for that may be ahead of time. Many insurance companies decided to get out of riskier fixed income in late 2008 and early 2009, because they could not handle the risk of default or their portfolio price declines, only to reenter the market at much higher prices a year or two later. For the most part, defaults, credit problems, and losses in fixed income come in bunches, so you will not only be forced to deal with your mistakes in the form of actual default losses, but also broad-based declines in prices due to the market's fear that defaults will occur for many more companies. The most difficult crisis is the one that has not yet been solved, and in late 2008 and early 2009, with high-yield bonds trading at extremely discounted prices and high-grade bonds plumbing the depths, it would have been easy to believe the worst. In fact, the worst seemed to be occurring on a daily basis, with no liquidity, fire-sale pricing, and the global financial system in disarray. Having bought a number of credits on the way down, I can tell you that even if you are "right" to buy a bond in the $70s, when it goes to $50 it doesn't feel very good.

At least buying a bond in the $70s (or $50s!) forces you, as the analyst, to recognize that there is a significant possibility of loss. More challenging is analysis of a bond at par or above par, where the presumption is that the credit is good. I always laugh at the presumption of precision within both bond and stock analyses. Precision is defined as the specificity or exactness of a number, whether or not it is right. Accuracy is really everyone's goal: Accuracy is defined as the result of a particular analysis being close to the correct figure, no matter how precisely defined that result is. One way to think about precision is the practice of drawing out calculations to hundredths of a percent, or a basis point. Bond investors fight about basis points all the time. But can anyone really presume precision about the likelihood of a very unlikely event? How likely is a bond to default? 1 percent? 2 percent? 2.07 percent? These are the calculations that investors are making all the time.

As we've discussed, though default losses in bonds and markdown losses in stocks are one kind of mistake and can hurt badly, investors can also be hurt by losses due to interest rate changes. While these are not "permanent," because a change in an interest rate changes a price, while the bond still will mature at par, it is undoubtedly the case that receiving a 3 percent coupon in a 6 percent yielding world *is* a permanent loss. The same limitations that investors confront with regard to individual issue analysis also exist in the analysis of macroeconomic fundamentals.

Given the laughable precision that is ever present in the market, the key to any analysis is the importance of being flexible in your thought process. Let's pick up the subject of mortgages again for a moment. Over the past decade, the boom and bust cycle of housing and the mortgage market has been breathtaking. Though I would argue that easy money was the real cause of the credit boom, an ancillary factor was the strongly held belief that housing prices could not decline. Though house prices had been going down in Japan for more than two decades, almost everyone believed that it couldn't happen in the U.S. As a result, a huge industry was built around satisfying the desire of every American to own a home, even if the mortgage borrower had no ability to repay. After all, if the borrower ran into trouble, he could always sell the home. AAA bonds were created based on that assumption. Most analysts did not have enough flexibility to imagine a world where prices went down. If they had, huge portions of their investment universe would have been, and ultimately were, quite mispriced. Ultimately, that flexible thought process will allow you, as the analyst of a company's situation and prospects, to consider a wider variety of potential outcomes. The gloomy analyst, Shakespeare's Hamlet, said: "There are more things in heaven and earth, Horatio/ Than are dreamt of in your philosophy." Certainly, a longer-term investment horizon and an understanding of your limits are helpful in avoiding Hamlet's fate.

TOP DOWN: THE MARKET ENVIRONMENT

The second point of analysis that Minsky's Financial Instability Hypothesis raises is the state of the overall market environment. Consider 2008 (which I know you probably have at great length, as have I). On the individual security basis, 2008 more than any year in any living investors' memory made clear that a bond may not return what is promised. Many bonds that were given the highest regard and rating by professionals at both asset managers and rating agencies effectively went from $100.00 to $0.00. But while this happens in almost any year, 2008 showed that entire asset classes can experience enormous stress. Once more, mortgages are the poster child for this. A formerly liquid, respected asset class is now nearly untouchable for most investors.

But it's not just at the security level or the asset class level that instability takes root in Minsky-esque fashion. The entire U.S. economy was caught up in a wave of optimism around housing finance. It seemed as though every other professional was becoming a real estate agent, builder, or investor. The building of too many houses financed by too much money had a meaningful effect on the growth of the U.S. economy as a whole. This isn't the mistake of a single group (like Wall Street bankers), but the collective and reinforcing actions of a huge portion of the country. Like it or not, we as human beings are prone to manias, and once we got done with dot-com stocks and Enron's energy trading techniques, we moved straight into housing finance. Especially given the large amounts of global liquidity sloshing around the system due to the energetic actions of the Federal Reserve and European Central Bank, among others, there are bound to be other manias and crashes. Certainly the current European sovereign crisis is another example.

PORTFOLIO CONSTRUCTION

I have spoken with many financial advisors who hate bond funds. Their view is that bond funds always blow up and never do what they are designed to do. After getting this far in the book, I hope you understand why this might be. But I believe it's possible to construct portfolios that might have a better chance of avoiding the fate of so many income-seeking investors, as long as you set expectations and time horizons appropriately.

Within the investment universe, bond fund managers are often described as perennially gloomy. When confronted with good news, fixed-income investors often recall Eeyore, the continually gloomy donkey from A.A. Milne's *Winnie-the-Pooh*. The biggest reason for this state of continual worry is that, as we've seen at the individual security level, bond investing is subject to asymmetric return. Still, investors sometimes believe that significant diversification will save them from price declines during periods of market stress.

It does not. Of course we can talk about how risky assets are correlated, and when there is stress in the system, that correlation increases. But perhaps more instructive is examining the actual results of a group of fixed-income portfolio managers. Looking at the distribution of returns for Morningstar's short-term bond category on a year by year basis, it's pretty clear that, in most years, bond investors receive more or less the same return given a somewhat similar set of investments. However, there are periods of significant stress (like 2008 and, to a lesser degree, 2011) where the difference between the best and worst performers was significant. Not only that, but in those stress periods the worst performers lost quite a bit, while in the less stressed period the best performers couldn't do enough to gain back those sorts of losses.

Taking significant risks in high-quality bond portfolios can lead to big losses. You don't want to own the stuff that's going to go up the most in good times unless you're prepared to ride it down in the bad times. Even supposing that good periods could make up for bad periods within the fixed income universe, most investors look toward their core fixed-income allocation for steady income and pricing. Sure, 2008 was extraordinary, but even in that time, with the extreme volatility of the market we saw, having a fund that lost as much as an equity fund is not part of a core bond allocation.

To put the risk another way, looking at "average" returns is not necessarily a good gauge of an investor's experience. Looking at the range of experience—the highs and lows—that investors have with a fund and when that happens is very important. When an investor allocates money to a core fixed-income strategy, she probably wants to have an anchor for income within her portfolio.

A final consideration around risk is how a particular fund or investment reacts with the rest of your portfolio. When looking for ballast for your portfolio in the form of a core fixed-income allocation, it is important to note the correlation between that portfolio and another key piece of many investors' asset allocations: equities. Low and negative correlation is a huge benefit in down markets.

In all, just examining returns over a certain time period, particularly a shorter period, is not enough to determine the quality of a given fixed-income portfolio. Because of negative skew (likelihood of negative outcomes and their disproportionate effect) as well as unwanted volatility, a portfolio that produces good total returns over a short period may not be the best place for investor dollars. Longer-term returns, combined with an examination of negative experiences within the portfolio, probably better qualify as appropriate indicators of quality. Looking to each investment's reaction to various markets and how they can form a balanced whole also is a key to successful investment.

If, as an investor, you're willing to take more risk and are less concerned about correlations, the fixed-income universe is full of a diverse set of risks. Prices may move in sync over short periods of time, but there is a truly wide variety of sources of income. With a $65 trillion global market, there are plenty of options. I'd suggest that, for those seeking a higher income stream and with a willingness to take additional risk to get it (a necessary combination), there is no reason to focus on one asset class. I've spent a significant amount of time on corporate credit as an example because so many investors gravitate toward that asset class when looking for yield. In fact, the term *high yield fund* refers directly to the asset class of speculative-grade corporate bonds. But interesting income exists in many places outside of junky corporates. An intelligent combination of nondollar fixed income, mortgages, junk bonds, stocks, and other income-producing securities will provide an internal diversification benefit from a default or permanent loss standpoint, even if it's difficult to escape correlation in the short term. As an example, the Australian Dollar is considered to be a commodity currency, given the reliance of the Australian economy on iron ore and coal production and export to growing economies in the Asian region. In an inflationary environment, the Australian Dollar is likely to appreciate relative to the U.S. Dollar. At the same time, interest rates on U.S. Treasuries are likely to rise in an inflationary environment. If a portfolio has both Australian Dollar exposure and exposure to U.S. Treasuries (or any high-quality U.S. Dollar–denominated bond), over a longer period of time movements in those two security types are likely to offset one another, while both provide income. There are no true hedges, but at least a portfolio that considers how a robust set of income sources can work together can have the potential for better outcomes in a large set of macroeconomic outcomes.

PERMANENCE OF CAPITAL

The right investment strategy is, in part, dependent on individual opportunities and market conditions, as we've seen. But the permanence of your capital is another factor that is less well appreciated. Just as liquidity in a given market can affect prices, your own capital liquidity is also important. As a fund manager, I'd like to believe that I have reasonably permanent capital. If my shareholders have long time horizons, the daily vicissitudes of the market will recede in importance and I will have the opportunity to manage their money through market cycles and through my own periods of underperformance (inevitable) and outperformance (I hope more frequent). But the reality is that the money I have to manage is only long term as long as my own performance remains reasonably good. My long-term performance is the most important aspect of my value creation for shareholders, but I don't get a chance to keep investing on their behalf if I have sufficiently ugly short- or medium-term returns. This is true for a tremendous number of participants in the market. Banks, certainly, are in this situation, even with the depositor protection that the FDIC provides. Hedge funds specifically try to structure their shareholder agreements so that there is a *lock-up period* wherein investors do not have the option to remove funds. Even if the lock-up period has expired, most hedge funds have a quarterly redemption policy that requires a significant notification period. Private equity is another investment construction that relies on longer-term lock-up and greater permanence of capital to achieve potentially greater returns with their leverage. Leveraged buyout funds are particularly notable in this way. Their whole existence depends on the asymmetry of bond returns versus equities, combined with a permanence of capital. In private equity, if you can convince yield-hungry investors to give you cheap money to buy a public company above where it is trading, and then just hold on to that investment for five to eight years, you can usually wait out a cycle. If the investment goes bad, you merely walk away or find a way to extract further capital from fearful bondholders. If it works out, bondholders are welcome to their 10 percent, but you've just made 100 or 200 percent. In addition, private equity investors make optionality work for them by taking out further debt for the sole purpose of "dividends" back to the private equity holder. It doesn't take too many wins to offset write downs on losers. But again, this is only possible because of the permanence of capital that private equity investment requires of its investors. The marks that investors in LBO funds were receiving were laughably high in 2008, but because investment agreements required further cash inflows to the private equity firm (contracts written in good times), there was no pressure by the LBO firm to liquidate.

When looking at investing for income, you need to consider your own capital permanence. I'm frequently asked, in this era of very low rates, especially on money market funds, if my funds are appropriate for a short-term investment. Usually a prospective investor needs the cash (for the purchase of a home, or a college tuition payment for a child) at some point in the reasonably near future, but the prospect of zero percent rates drives them to consider a longer-term fund for a shorter-term time horizon. This is a recipe for disaster. Impressive relative returns are available to any investor who has greater staying power: Many studies detail the poor performance of investors in funds relative to the funds themselves. Having an appropriate time horizon, and for riskier ventures, assuring your personal permanence of capital, will nearly always increase your returns. It's a great feeling to be happy when markets are down, because you have a better opportunity set and you are confident in your capital base. Part of understanding the myriad of security and market risks that I've detailed throughout this book is to help provide that confidence.

REFLEXIVITY

I think markets, and the securities that make up those markets, are impossible to model with any great accuracy. That doesn't mean that creating a future cash flow projection is a bad idea. It's important to try to understand what drives a particular investment. I spend an inordinate amount of time thinking about the gritty details of each bond or stock that I buy. The fundamental details of a company, say, or a mortgage, can to a degree be considered in the absence of the broader market environment.

But markets represent a system that changes when the participants who make up a market interact with it. George Soros termed this idea reflexivity.[3] The most obvious example of this is when you buy a stock. The act of purchasing that share of stock takes away one share that was available for sale at a certain price. If that is the last share of that stock available there, the next willing seller is only willing to transact at a higher price. So your action of purchasing stock changes the price of the stock. *Transactions costs* are often ignored by models of market behavior for this reason. But we've seen throughout our discussion here that these sorts of effects are impossible to ignore. The market actions in mortgage and corporate lending leading up to the 2008–2009 recession underline the idea that lenders' and borrowers' actions affected the market in exactly the way that Minsky's Financial Instability Hypothesis contemplates. On the face of it, the idea that the behavior of market participants affects the market is not very surprising or odd. But that means that modeling that behavior becomes much less straightforward. I hope I've been able to make clear that markets are made up of people making very suboptimal decisions, due to both their own psychology and the inevitably imperfect construction of the market itself.

The very reflexivity we've discussed makes me concerned about the valuation of income-producing securities and the short-term viability of income strategies, given the extreme demand in the market today. I've tried to detail all of the reasons why investors frequently fail to achieve their desired outcomes from a collection of yeldy securities. I would expect that we'll continue to see the same mistakes over and over again, just as the subprime mortgage crisis morphed into a banking crisis, which has again re-emerged as a European sovereign crisis. I don't *want* to see a crisis caused by an excessive desire for yield, but we've seen it before and we will certainly see it again. Market values change when we buy and sell, and the sheer weight of money pursuing bonds and dividend-paying stocks is bound to create volatility. All I can do is try to navigate the volatility for my shareholders and try to help investors navigate it similarly. Of course there is the thought that my advice, if correct, will change the market as well. But frankly, the fixation with yield and the pursuit of short-term returns is so innate in the marketplace that a library of books and how-to manuals wouldn't make a dent.

CONCLUSION

Throughout this book I've tried to illustrate the mechanisms of both income-producing instruments and the markets for those instruments. Neither is perfect, but then again neither is any analyst (a fact I continue to demonstrate with considerable frequency). Trying to get income from your investments is, in my opinion, a difficult task given the seductive nature of "yield" and the asymmetry of fixed-income investment. The current market environment, where rates are extraordinarily low and both dramatic inflation and debilitating deflation are possible, doesn't make the task of income investing any easier. Plus it's likely that, at some point, the proverbial cabbie who was giving dot-com stock tips in 2000 and real-estate tips in 2006 might be touting dividend-paying stocks before too long (at least for a time).

Ultimately, I believe many platitudes of investment hold true. Invest with an appropriate time horizon (longer is usually more productive). Buy when everyone else is selling. Sell when everyone else is buying. But away from the age-old exhortation to "buy low and sell high," there are some new ideas that might help. Try to understand the risks of what you hold, so that you can be confident in holding it. Don't get anchored on a yield number. Try to find investments that expose you to optionality on the upside instead of just downside, or at least provide you a significant margin of safety on the downside. Don't trust fancy models (or those bearing them), including ones that you yourself can produce. Recognize that markets are structured to blow up, but your investments don't have to be. All of this is easier said than done, a fact that I know from trying to execute these ideas on a daily basis. But the pages of the preceding analysis and argument are designed to try to provide insight into *why* these investment truisms work and what specifically you can do. Understanding the difficulty of the task in front of you is better than blindly taking risk and hoping for a reward. The risk and the reward are both uncertain, but that's what makes it interesting.

Good luck.

NOTES

Chapter 1

1. John D. Rockefeller, BrainyQuote.com, Xplore Inc., 2012. http://www.brainyquote.com/quotes/quotes/j/johndrock129792.html, accessed May 4, 2012.

2. "U.S. Stocks Decline, Erase Yearly Gain as S&P 500 Moves Least Since 1947," Ksenia Galouchko and Lu Wang, Bloomberg News, 12/31/11.

3. Tversky, A. and Kahneman, D. 1974. "Judgment under Uncertainty: Heuristics and Biases." *Science,* 185, 1124–1130.

Chapter 2

1. Graeber, David, 2011, *Debt: The First 5,000 Years,* Melville House Publishing, pp. 64–65.

2. Ibid, p. 46.

3. Bureau of Labor Statistics. www.bls.gov.

4. Bullard, James, 2010, "Seven Faces of "The Peril," http://research.stlouisfed.org/econ/bullard/pdf/SevenFacesFinalJul28.pdfhttp://research.stlouisfed.org/econ/bullard/pdf/SevenFacesFinalJul28.pdf.

5. www.federalreserve.gov/boarddocs/speeches/2002/20021121/default.htm.

6. Greenspan, Alan, 2010, "U.S. Debt and the Greece Analogy," *Wall St. Journal,* June 18, http://online.wsj.com/article/ NA_WSJ_PUB:SB10001424052748704198004575310962 247772540.html.

7. Bernanke, Ben, Testimony to Congress, July 21, 2010.

Chapter 3

1. www.standardandpoors.com/ratings/articles/en/us/?article Type=HTML&assetID=1245302234237.

2. Reinhart, Carmen, and Rogoff, Kenneth, 2009, *This Time Is Different,* Princeton University Press.

3. Grant, James, 1992, *Money of the Mind,* Noonday Press, p. 173.

4. www.ncsl.org/documents/fiscal/StateBalancedBudget Provisions2010.pdf.

5. Money Trust Investigation of Financial and Monetary Conditions in the United States Under House Resolutions Nos. 429 and 504. Part 15, December 19, 1912. p. 1084.

6. v2.moodys.com/cust/content/content.ashx?source= StaticContent/Free%20pages/Credit%20Policy%20 Research/documents/current/2006200000425249.pdf.

7. www.standardandpoors.com/ratings/articles/en/ us/?assetID=1245207201119.

Chapter 4

1. Taleb, Nassim, 2007, *The Black Swan,* Random House.

2. www.inbest.co.il/images/black_swans.pdf.

3. http://www.risk.net/risk-magazine/news/2103622/myron-scholes-predicts-golden-age-quants.

4. Emanuel Derman, 2010, *Models. Behaving. Badly,* Free Press.

5. Kahneman, Daniel, 2011, *Thinking, Fast and Slow,* Farrar, Strauss and Giroux.

6. Ibid.

7. Taleb, Nassim, 2007.

8. Author's personal conversation with Jared Dillian.

9. Reinhart, Carmen, and Rogoff, Kenneth, 2009.

Chapter 5

1. Robert D. Arnott and Clifford S. Asness, "Surprise! Higher Dividends = Higher Earnings Growth?" *Financial Analysts Journal,* Jan.–Feb. 2003. Data analyzed: 1946–2001.

Chapter 6

1. Grant, James, pp. 53–54.

2. Galbraith, John Kenneth, 1975, *Money: Whence It Came, Where It Went,* Houghton Mifflin.

3. von Mises, Ludwig, 1934, *The Theory of Money and Credit,* Yale University Press.

4. Bagehot,Walter, 1910, *Lombard Street: A Description of the Money Market,* Cosimo Classics.

Chapter 7

1. Grant, Jim, "Money of the Mind," p. 54.

2. Minsky, Hyman, May 1992, *The Financial Instability Hypothesis,* Working Paper No 74, http://www.levyinstitute. org/pubs/wp74.pdf.

3. Soros, George, "The Alchemy of Finance," Simon and Schuster, 1988, pp. 27–48.

INDEX

ABS (asset-backed securities), 94–95
   (*See also* Mortgages)
Accuracy, 191
Agency mortgages, 85–86, 111
American Airlines bankruptcy, 68
American banks, 180–183
Anchoring, 9, 10, 203
Annuities, 137–138
Argentina, 58–59
Asian Financial Crisis, 113
Asset value, 77–78
Asset-backed securities (ABS), 94–95
   (*See also* Mortgages)
Assets, 166, 188
AT&T, 49–50
Australia, 197
Auto loans, 94–95

Baby boomers:
   retirement of, 33
   spending by, 6
Bagehot, Walter, 179
Balance sheets, 52, 73, 166–168
Bank CDs, 138
Bank loan funds, 142–144
Bank of America, 172
Bankruptcy, 76–77, 136–137, 143
Banks, 165–183
   balance sheets of, 38, 166–168
   and Credit Default Swaps, 82
   European vs. American, 180–183
   government's relationship with, 179–180
   investment world's perception of, 165
   as investors, 168–172
   and leverage, 139–140, 178
   and liquidity, 173–179
   and optionality, 106–107
   sale of assets by, 188
   and solvency, 173–179
   and yield curves, 26
Barclays Aggregate Index, 69
Basel regime, 181
Bear markets, 173
Bear Stearns, 171
Bell curve, 105, 113, 117, 118f, 170 (*See also* Normal distributions)
Bernanke, Ben, 39–40, 42, 79
Bids, 46

Black, Fischer, 104
The Black Swan (Nassim Taleb), 117, 125
Black Swans and Market Timing (Javier Estrada), 119
Black-Scholes equation, 104, 105, 117
"The Blob" (risk), 127
BNP Paribas, 177
Bond above par, 190
Bond at par, 190
Bond fund managers, 194–195
Bond portfolios, 70–71
Bondholders, 107–108, 107f, 111
Bonds, 43–83
   asset-backed, 82–83
   asymmetric returns on, 12–13, 79–80, 99, 106
   and balance sheets, 52
   corporate, 67–82
   credit ratings of, 47–51
   general obligation, 65–66
   government, 52–67
   high yield, 69
   junk, 69, 79
   movement in prices of, 7
   municipal, 62–67
   overview of, 18–19
   revenue, 66
   safety with, 116–117
   simplicity of, 15
   sovereign-government, 56–62
   stocks vs., 44–46
   tax-exempt, 62–63
   yield on, 98–101, 149–150
   (*See also specific types*)
Book value (*see* Equity capital)
Borrowers, 189
Bottom up analysis, 189–193
Brazil, 59, 60
"Breaking the buck," 139
Broker-dealers, 46, 47
Bullard, James, 38

California state bonds, 62
Call options, 102–104, 104f, 110
Capacity (credit risk analysis), 72
Capital:
   equity, 86, 167
   permanence of, 198–200

Capitalization (cap) rate, 93
Carry trades, 121
Cash alternative, 141
CDOs (Collateralized Debt Obligations), 92
CDS (Credit Default Swaps), 80–82
Change, 19–23
Character (credit risk analysis), 72
China, 37
China Mobile, 159–160
Citigroup, 172
CMBS (commercial mortgage-backed securities), 92–93
Cognitive biases, 9
Collateral, 72–73, 77–78
Collateralized Debt Obligations (CDOs), 92
Commercial mortgage-backed securities (CMBS), 92–93
Conditions, economic (*see* Economic conditions)
Confidence, 97, 178 (*See also* Overconfidence)
Conservatorship, 86
Consumer Price Index (CPI), 35, 56
Convergence trade, 130
Convertible bonds, 134–136
Corporate bond spreads, 111–112, 112*f*
Corporate bonds, 67–82
    as contracts, 12
    and Credit Default Swaps, 80–82
    credit ratings of, 50, 78–80
    credit risk with, 70–76
    default rates on, 129
    effects of market stress on, 113–114
    as fixed-income security, 44
    risk with, 106
    trouble with, 76–78
Correlation, 126–129, 195, 196
Cost of money, 23–28, 104 (*See also* Interest rates)
Coverage ratio (EBITDA to interest payments), 74–75
CPI (Consumer Price Index), 35, 56
Credit analysis, 189–190
Credit Default Swaps (CDS), 80–82
Credit enhancement, 87, 90–92
Credit metrics, 73–76
Credit rating agencies, 47–50, 182
Credit ratings, 47–51
    of corporate bonds, 50, 78–80
    for money market funds, 139
Credit risk:
    with corporate bonds, 70–76
    with floating rate funds, 142
Credit-card loans, 94
Cyclicality (of company), 75

Debt:
    government, 111, 130, 181
    history of money and, 15–17
    inevitability of, 147
    and mortgage refinancing, 83
Debt metrics, 74
Debt to GDP ratio:
    and feedback loop, 131, 132
    and global debt, 58
    and growth, 59–60
    of Italy, 133
    of Japan, 57
Default:
    probability of, 49, 78
    soft, 111
Default risk, 68
Deflation, 37–41
Demand, 26, 27, 186
Depository banks, 171–172
Derman, Emanuel, 123
Developed markets, 58, 60
Developing markets, 37, 58–59
Dillian, Jared, 127
Disbursement stage, 6
Discount brokerages, 44–45
Diversification, 71, 101
Dividend rate, 105
Dividends:
    on equities, 149–158, 156*t*
    tendency to forget about, 7
Dotcom bubble, 11, 194
Dow Jones Industrial Average, 173
Duration:
    of assets and liabilities, 188
    interest rate, 142
    with mortgages, 84–85
    overview of, 19–23, 21*f*
    short, 141–143

EBITDA (Earnings Before Interest, Taxes, Depreciation, and Amortization), 74–75
Economic conditions:
    analysis of, 189
    in credit risk analysis, 73
    employment conditions, 31–35, 34*f*
    gross domestic product growth, 36–37
    inflation, 35–36
    and interest rates, 27–28
    and optionality, 120–122
    in top down analysis, 193–194
Economic variables, 31–37
Emerging markets, 59, 61
Employment conditions, 31–35, 34*f*
Endowments, 6
Enron, 11, 68, 113, 177, 194

Equilibrium, 186–187
Equities, 145–163
    and bond yields, 149–150
    dividends on, 149–158, 156*t*
    global, 153–154
    growth with, 155–157
    high yield vs. growing yield with, 158–160
    income from stocks, 147, 160–163
    optionality and volatility with, 148
    overlooking of, 145
    potential income from, 146–148
    (*See also* Stocks)
Equity capital, 86, 167
Equity markets, 43, 44
Equity value, 107
Estrada, Javier, 119–120
Euro, 59, 130–131
Eurobond, 51
European banks, 180–183
European Central Bank, 51, 60, 194
European sovereign debt crisis, 51,
    130–131, 194
Eurozone countries, 58, 130, 182
Ex-Bills, 53
Expectations, 10
    readjustment of, 100–101
    in yield curves, 25

Fannie Mae, 85
"Fat tails," 117–118, 124
FDIC, 138, 171
Fear, 11, 113
Federal Reserve, 28–31
    and banks, 172, 179
    buying of commercial paper by, 75
    economic variables influenced by, 31, 35
    energetic actions of, 194
    and inflation, 39–41
    lowering of rates by, 60
    raising of front-end rates by, 113
    and U.S. Treasuries, 54–56
Feedback loops, 129–133
FICO score, 87
Financial crises, 125
Financial crisis of 2008/2009, 113, 128–129,
    173–174, 193–194
Financial Instability Hypothesis, 186–189,
    201
Financial models:
    and asymmetry of returns, 11
    imperfect nature of, 122–123, 201, 203
Financial stocks, 155, 161
First loss, 88
Fixed annuities, 138
Fixed income:
    optionality in, 106–111

psychology of, 125
Fixed income-securities:
    mysteries with, 15
    popular view of, 43–44
    yields on, 30–31
    (*See also specific headings*)
Flat yield curves, 25
Floating rate funds, 142
Foreign government bonds
    (*see* Government bonds)
Foundations, 6
"Four Cs," 71–73, 75, 78
Freddie Mac, 85

Gains, 125–126
Galbraith, John Kenneth, 169
Gauss, Johann Carl Friedrich, 118
Gaussian distribution, 118, 118*f*
GDP (gross domestic product) growth, 36–38
General obligation bonds (GOs), 65–66
German bonds, 56–57, 60
Global debt market, 57–58
Global equities, 153–154, 154*f*
Global trade, 37
Goldman Sachs, 46, 172
GOs (general obligation bonds), 65–66
Government bonds, 52–67
    municipal, 62–67
    optionality with, 110–111
    sovereign-government bonds, 56–62
    U.S. Treasuries (*see* U.S. Treasuries)
Government debt, 111, 130, 181
Government Sponsored Entities (GSEs), 85
Governments, 179–180
Graeber, David, 16–17
Grant, Jim, 61–62, 169, 185
Great Depression, 173
"Greater fool" concept, 11, 18–19
Greece, 130–133
Greed, 11
Greenspan, Alan, 40–41
Gross domestic product (GDP) growth,
    36–38
Growing yield, 158–160
Growth, 155–157
GSEs (Government Sponsored Entities), 85

Hawthorne, Nathaniel, 5
Hedge finance, 187
Hedge funds, 134, 176
Hedged fixed-income funds, 144
High yield, 141–143, 158–160
High yield bonds, 69
High yield funds, 197
Home prices, 37–38
Housing market, 83 (*See also* Mortgages)

In the money options, 103
Income, 98, 102, 160–163
Income investing, 5–14
    asymmetry of returns in, 11–14
    concept of, 5–6
    slow movement of, 6–9
    yield and investor psychology in, 9–11
Inflation, 14, 35–36
    deflation vs., 37–41
    and employment, 32, 35–36
    and stocks, 161
    and U.S. Treasuries, 55
Information technology sector, 154
Insurance companies, 64–65, 87, 137, 190
Interest rate duration, 142
Interest rate risk, 21, 22
Interest rates:
    basic economics of, 26–28
    and duration, 20–21
    set by Federal Reserve, 29–31
Interest-bearing debt, 16
International Swaps and Derivatives
    Association (ISDA), 80
Intesa San Paulo, 182–183
Inverted yield curves, 25
Investment-grade securities, 49
Investor psychology:
    flaws in, 123
    gains and losses in, 125–126
    and yield, 9–11
ISDA (International Swaps and Derivatives
    Association), 80
Italian bonds, 57
Italy, 60, 133, 181

Japan, 38, 55, 153
Japanese bonds, 57
Japanese Government Bond (JGB), 57
J.P. Morgan, 171
Junk bonds, 69, 79, 116

Kahneman, Daniel, 9, 123–125
Keynes, John Maynard, 165

LBO (see Leveraged buyout)
Lehman Brothers, 11, 171, 172, 177, 181
Leverage:
    with agency mortgages, 86
    and banks, 139–140, 178
    with convertible bonds, 135
    with Credit Default Swaps, 82
    shift in attitude toward, 175
Leverage ratio (Total Debt to EBITDA),
    74, 77
Leveraged buyout (LBO), 152, 181, 189
Leveraged longs, 121

Liabilities, 166, 188
LIBOR (see London Interbank Offered Rate)
Life insurance companies, 26
Linkers, 56
Liquidity, 46, 67, 173–179
Liquidity preference, 24, 30
Loan structure, 87
Loan to value ratio, 87
Loans:
    auto, 94–95
    credit-card, 94
    subprime, 188 (See also Subprime
        mortgage crisis)
Lombard Street (Walter Bagehot), 179
London Interbank Offered Rate (LIBOR),
    114, 115, 142
Long Term Capital Management (LTCM),
    121–122
Losses, 125–126

Macroeconomics, 192
Manias, 194
Margin of safety, 116, 189–193
Market conditions (see Economic
    conditions)
Market depth, 174
Markham, Beryl, 97
Marlowe, Christopher, 15
Maturity, 18–19, 142
MBS (see Mortgage-backed securities)
Media, 6
Merrill Lynch, 172
Merton, Robert, 104, 107
Metrics, 73–76
MF Global, 181
Minsky, Hyman, 186–189, 201
Models (see Financial models)
Models. Behaving. Badly (Emanuel
    Derman), 123
Money, debt and, 15–17
Money market funds, 29, 99–100, 139–140
Morgan, J.P., 72
Morgan Stanley, 172
Morningstar ratings, 195
Mortgage-backed securities (MBS):
    commercial, 92–93
    credit ratings of, 51
    optionality with, 108–110
Mortgages, 82–93
    agency, 85–86, 111
    boom and bust cycle of, 192
    commercial mortgage-backed securities,
        92–93
    nonagency, 85–87, 89
    residential, 73, 83–89, 187, 188
    (See also Subprime mortgage crisis)

Municipal bonds, 62–67
  demise of insurers for, 64–65
  overview of, 62–63
  types of, 65–67

NAIRU (Non-Accelerating Rate of
    Unemployment), 32
"Naked" Credit Default Swaps, 81
National Association of Securities Dealers
    (NASD), 45
Negative skew, 196
Negotiability, 174
Net interest margin (NIM), 167
"Netting out," 82
New Hampshire state bonds, 62
New York City bonds, 62–63
News media, 6
Nikkei average, 173
NIM (net interest margin), 167
Non-Accelerating Rate of Unemployment
    (NAIRU), 32
Nonagency (private label) mortgages,
    85–87, 89
Normal distributions, 105, 117–126, 118f, 170

"Odd lots," 45
Offers, 46
"Operation Twist," 39
Optionality, 97–144
  asset classes and products illustrating,
      134–144
  concept of, 97–98
  correlation in, 126–129
  effects of, 111–116
  with equities, 148
  feedback loops in, 129–133
  in fixed income, 106–111
  and normal distributions, 105, 117–126
  overview of, 102–106
  yield as cushion in, 116–117
  and yield as measure of return, 98–102
Options:
  defined, 102
  overview of, 102–106
  (See also Optionality)
Out of the money options, 103
"Over the counter" trading, 45
Overconfidence, 123–124, 126, 139, 182

Panic, financial, 166, 171, 172, 178
Past performance, 10
Ponzi finance, 187–189
Portfolio risk, 185, 195–196
Portfolios:
  bond, 70–71
  construction of, 194–198

diversified, 101
ideal, 185
and permanence of capital, 198–200
PPI (Producer Price Index), 35
Precision, 191
"Preferred habitat" theory, 26
Preferred stock, 136–137
Premiums, 98
Prepayments, 84
Price change equation, 22
Private label mortgages (see Nonagency
    mortgages)
Producer Price Index (PPI), 35
Projection deals, 188–189
Put options, 102–103

"Quantitative easing," 54

Recession, 157
Recovery value, 99
"Refi wave," 83
Refinancing, 83, 108–109
Reflexivity, 200–202
Reinhart, Carmen, 59, 131
Reinvestment risk, 21, 22
Residential mortgages, 73, 83–89, 187, 188
Returns, asymmetric, 11–14, 79–80,
    99, 106
Revenue bonds, 66
Reward, 189
Risk:
  in analysis, 189
  credit, 70–76, 142
  default, 68
  interest rate, 21, 22
  portfolio, 185, 195–196
  reinvestment, 21, 22
  shifting of, 176
Risk distribution model, 177
Risk on/risk off environment, 127
Risk-free bonds, 23
Risk-free state, 104
Rockefeller, John D., 5
Rogoff, Kenneth, 59, 131
Roll-overs, market, 75–76
Ryon, Chris, 117

Sarbanes-Oxley Act, 178
Scholes, Myron, 104, 122
Shadow banks, 176
Short-termism, 6–8, 121, 143, 147
"Smart money," 146
"Soft default," 111
Solvency, 173–179
Sovereign debt (see Government debt)
Sovereign-government bonds, 56–62

S&P (see Standard & Poor's)
Speculative finance, 187
Speculative-grade securities, 49
Spread duration, 23
Standard & Poor's (S&P), 6, 53, 155–157,
    156t, 173
State guaranty schemes, 137
Statistics, 118
Steep yield curves, 25
Stock holders, 107–108, 107f
Stocks, 15
    bonds vs., 44–46
    dividend-paying, 149–153, 151t, 152t
    financial, 155, 161
    income from, 147, 160–163
    and inflation, 161
    returns on, 105
    yield on, 100
    (See also Equities)
Strike price, 103, 106
"Structured products," 175
Subprime loans, 188
Subprime mortgage crisis, 89–92, 114–115,
    129–130, 174
Success, 97
Supply, 26, 27, 186
Swaps, Credit Default, 80–82

Taleb, Nassim, 117, 125
Taxes, 33, 52
Tax-exempt bonds, 62–63
T-Bills, 53 (See also U.S. Treasuries)
T-Bonds, 53 (See also U.S. Treasuries)
Telecom industry, 161
Thinking, Fast and Slow (Daniel
    Kahneman), 123–125
This Time is Different (Carmen Reinhart
    and Kenneth Rogoff), 59, 131
Time, 19–23 (See also Duration)
TIPS (Treasury Inflation Protected
    Securities), 56
T-Notes, 53 (See also U.S. Treasuries)
Top down analysis, 193–194
Trade Reporting and Compliance Engine
    (TRACE), 45
"Trader's option," 178
Tranching, 87–89, 88f, 91–92
Transaction costs, 201
Treasuries (see U.S. Treasuries)
Treasury Inflation Protected Securities
    (TIPS), 56
Tversky, Amos, 9

Ultra short funds, 141–142, 144
Underemployment, 33–35

Unemployment rate, 32–35
United States government, 132
Upside optionality, 148 (See also
    Optionality)
Upside volatility, 148, 149
U.S. Bureau of Labor Statistics, 32
U.S. Department of Commerce, 36
U.S. Treasuries:
    backing of mortgages with, 85–86, 111
    as benchmarks, 63
    credit ratings of, 51
    and Federal Reserve, 54–56
    frequent trading of, 46
    historic yields on, 13f
    and inflation, 40–41
    margin of safety with, 117
    in November 2008, 128
    overview of, 52–54
    safety of, 60
    slowly rising yields on, 113
    volume of, 47
U6 rate, 34–35

Value at Risk (VaR), 170–171
Verizon, 45–46
Vermont, 65
Vintage, 87
VIX index, 112, 112f, 120
Volatility:
    of bonds, 101
    effect on fixed-income investments,
        111
    with equities, 148
    importance of, 149
    in income investing, 8, 10
    and market stress, 113
    of options, 103
    unwanted, 196
    in Value at Risk, 170–171
Volcker Rule, 47
Voltaire, 145
Von Mises, Ludwig, 173–175

Windstream, 158–160
Worldcom, 11, 113, 177
Wyatt, Thomas, 43

Yield:
    as bad measure of return, 98–102
    as cushion, 116–117
    high vs. growing, 158–160
    and investor psychology, 9–11
Yield curve:
    and the Federal Reserve, 29–30
    overview of, 23–26, 24f, 24t